In Search
of Solitude

ICCS
PRESS

In Search
of Solitude

Living the Classic
Christian Hours of Prayer

Thomas C. Oden

ICCS Press
NEW HAVEN, CONNECTICUT

ICCS PRESS

In Search of Solitude
Copyright © 2020 by Thomas C. Oden

Originally published 2010 by Zondervan

Requests for information should be addressed to:

ICCS Press, *616 Prospect St, New Haven, CT 06511*

ISBN 978-1-62428-012-2

Cover design: speersdesign.com
Interior design: Sherri L. Hoffman

CONTENTS

The scene:
lakeside at Egret Point

The characters:
you, her, me

The time:
beginning before dawn of the first day,
continuing for seven weeks

Entrance:
all characters

PROLOGUE

When the world is sleeping it is the Hour of Vigils.
When the world is awakening it is the Hour of Lauds.
When the world is working it is the Hour of Terce.
When the world is relaxing it is the Hour of Sext.
When the world is struggling to survive it is the Hour of None.
When the world is bathing in the glory of sunset it is the Hour
of Vespers.
When the world is yielding and retiring it is the Hour of
Compline.

Scriptural Focus:
"Seven times a day I praise you."
Psalm 119:164

———— INTRODUCTION————

Welcome to Egret Point

Egret Point is a cove and a rock dwelling on a peninsular point. I stand on the Point to look out from a sheltered place on to the blue cove. This is the setting where I have enjoyed the changing seasons, observed living creatures, studied, and labored.

The Point is a little-noticed, out-of-the-way green patch on a wide, dry prairie. The Point overlooks a moving stream that forms a sudden lake. The stream bends north here. From this point I feast eyes daily on a wide stream to my left and a flourishing lake to my right.

Here I live with water birds and wildlife and wildflowers in abundance. This gentle turn of the stream is called Goose Bend. Canadian geese come and go, and many stay all year. My hermitage is on a promontory jutting out into the lake.

A large weeping willow anchors the corner of the Point. Its supple branches bow down low to touch the water. Here the geese gather to feed on native grasses. Here the mother geese come annually to lay their precious eggs, keep them warm, and nurture goslings into little furry balls of waddling life.

These meditations arise out of this specific panorama. My intent is not simply to describe this natural environment, though I delight in doing that. Rather, my hope is to hold my life up in God's presence every hour of every day I'm given. This is where these meditations on the hours of light and darkness were conceived and warmed to birth like nested eggs.

Take some time to walk around. Notice how still the geese are in the water this evening. It is a secluded place where nature's time prevails over human time, where voices of gulls trump human voices, where God's presence touches all human presence.

You are among the few who have visited Egret Point on Goose Bend.

Called to the Inconspicuous

After an active life I am called to be here with these companions beside these still waters.

I say it softly since it is said without her. This is my place, not better than another, just the place to which I was called to bear this tranquil testimony. Here I am called to be myself in time within this wide horizon.

From this spot I still circle the globe in imagination, just as I have flown round it in fact many times before. I have lived an eventful and engaged life.

This is not a place to which many are called, though others are always welcomed. They must discover for themselves that particular place to which they are called to ponder the mystery of life in time.

Nor do I imply that this solitary life is meant to be followed as a rule by anyone else, and certainly not everyone. Like celibacy, this is not a life to which every soul is fitted. But the solitary life is a way open to some to allow freedom to ponder.

In the postteaching years of my life I have been challenged to live more fully what I have taught. I came here to meld prayer and study, worship and work. Through each tone or color of each hour of light or shadow, this is my desire.

Though most can state how many years they have lived, no one can tell how many days they have left. Each day provides time to be savored.

What am I doing at Egret Point? Nothing of importance, but everything needful. Here I read, garden, breathe, keep in touch with dear friends, and live alone, yet not really alone. I seldom feel the pain of loneliness or despair. I am with her in spirit and memory, because I am with you, Lord, in reality and in truth. You, me, and her. This is what this conversation is about.

What to Expect

Here is a collection of meditations that record inward recognitions on a spiritual pilgrimage. They are not intended to be a series of lessons or a handbook for daily prayer or an objective report of seven cycles of daily prayers. They offer only a window into a unique personal inward journey of unspecified length.

They can be read straight through or as an incremental voyage of discovery within a sevenfold timeframe of days extending over a seven-week period. Each day of each week conforms with the classic "hours" of spiritual formation.

In this way I have traveled through time leaving a weather-beaten record of a journey you now hold in your hands. I have pondered whether to tell it at all or, if at all, to tell it just as it happened without embellishment. Now I know I must tell it just as it happened.

As a writer I have long wanted to share this journey. But until I discovered the canonical hours, I did not know how to make it clear to anyone but myself.

The classic hours have served as a trellis on which to display the blossoms of my trumpet vines. Or something like a high scaffold on which to hang glimpses of life with God, as if painting upon a precipitous vertical space.

I've long known that I was called to take note of my own daily spiritual formation, but I was at a loss to see how this might impinge upon any other pilgrim along the way. I have been writing these glimpses on slips of paper, napkins, notepads, margins of newspapers, airline disposable bags, anything handy, for decades. They were not written for others but as notes for myself, mostly to God, and often attuned to her. Her? I will explain.

Only after some misgivings did I even grasp the possibility that they might be found interesting or useful or worth mentioning to anyone else. But until I found my way into the canonical hours I could not think of any way I could share them with others who might, for whatever reason, be drawn toward them as one happens accidentally to overhear a private conversation.

Then I began to pray the hours according to the Benedictine way of the fifth century AD. This pattern adapted for the European world an even more ancient African desert (proto-Coptic) pattern of daily prayer. I then realized that all along the inner coherence of these meditations belonged within a structure of time long known by Christian believers — the classic canonical hours.

The signpost here reads: study, prayer, silence.

Why silence? And if silence, then why would I break silence to speak of silence? This is a silence I do not break but extend by sharing. Silence is fully itself without being spoken. It does not need human speech to be experienced, as prayer does not need sounds in order to be prayed.

The active life has taught me to value the grace of quietness. The Greeks called this *hesuchia* — yieldedness, obedience, tranquility. It listens.

I am called to listen to the quietness of Egret Point. This is especially so when her voice is silent — that soothing voice so gently remembered.

With St. Anthony in the Desert

The awareness of this vocation conspicuously entered my consciousness at a particular moment long ago. In an instant I knew what I was to do.

I was traveling into the far eastern desert of Egypt. Through many hours of rutted passage, amid an endless treeless desert, I was intent upon visiting the isolated place where St. Anthony had fled from his privileged life to become the unlikely founder of solitary monasticism in the third century.

After long barren stretches of emptiness, I came to the Red Sea, turned south with Mount Clysma on my right and the narrow sea on my left. At length I came to an isolated turn on a dusty road toward the mountains. There I climbed a steep walk a thousand feet up to the Cave of St. Anthony of the Desert.

The well-worn path led to the place where Anthony spent so many years of his life. He lived to be 105 (251 to 356 AD). I was about half that many years. My pace slowed in the ascent.

With candle in hand I squeezed into a slender rocky cell, barely tall enough to stand up straight. The rock walls were basalt black.

The cell, a natural cleft in the rocks, reached a hundred feet deep into the heart of the silent mountain. At the far end of the cave was a small room, hand hewn of rock, hardly large enough to be called a dwelling, maybe eight feet wide. As I rested my head on the rounded stone that served as Anthony's pillow, I knew. I was recognizing some unknown part of myself that had long awaited this moment.

In that cave with the tiny light flickering off dark walls, I realized that something had been missing in all of my previous married and family life—silence and solitude. Solitude was what I had most dreaded. But there I found solitude, or was found by it, with my head on a hard black rock, at peace with myself in a way not known before. There I found a central clue to the puzzle of my life.

Exactly here was where seeds of ancient ascetic Christianity took root: in a wet cave on a rugged mountain in a dry and empty desert landscape. St. Anthony lived there many years alone. In time a gathering of his uninvited disciples formed at the base of the mountain. In the valley there was, and still is, a spring and a garden.

Not long after that I lost the one I love. Death took her in the night. I plunged into darkness.

After her passing I found my way unexpectedly to Egret Point. I soon realized that this was a place where I wanted to be in sync with time.

I was longing for some place to recover the peace that had flown away with her. I came back to the arid place where I was born—a thirsty prairie setting. This is where a passageway appeared.

Ordered Solitude

Amid long silences on Egret Point, I discovered a secret long obscured from my modern Protestant memory—the observance of *the hours*.

The pattern was set for me while traveling with Avery Dulles years ago in Israel. He was barely able to squeeze his long legs into the cramped mini-car I was driving. Over many days I noted how consistently he observed the hours—inconspicuously, as a practiced daily habit of prayer. This prompted me to obtain the same daily order and begin this practice.

Seven times a day in the light-dark cycle I learned to come before God, as had so many who had gone so much deeper than I into the mystery of time. This pattern follows the psalmist's sevenfold ordering of the times of prayer: "Seven times a day I praise you" (Psalm 119:164).

I learned that if I did not pursue a life of prayer regularly ordered on a timely basis, I would fall short of my calling to simplicity. So it was in my case through a specific arrangement of time that I have found my life to be little by little illumined. This is what these meditations mirror.

It was through these set-aside times that I found my way slowly through darkness to dim illumination; then, by grace, to clearer forms of recognition. I was being drawn by grace toward life with God. It came inconspicuously, like dew dripping from leaves.

Invited by God to "ask that I might receive," I asked. With all my heart I asked. To my surprise I began to receive. It was like a dim light shining through the mist that was settling on lowlands.

Through this life of ordered prayer, I learned to come ever closer to God's great presence entering my little time.

I do not feel cast away. I have freely chosen to be here. I am not neglected by others. They call when they need me. I love being with others. I love those times of being with myself. I am not escaping from the real world. It is present before my eyes every day in every blade of grass.

After a full and active life of university teaching, my day job had become an editor and commentator on early Christian texts. Here I have labored silently in the scriptorium of the *Ancient Christian Commentary on Scripture* and its successor projects. The *Commentary* consists of twenty-nine volumes of translations of writers of the first eight centuries from Latin, Greek, and Syriac into modern languages.

My vision narrowed to here and now. In doing so, I discovered the wider world and long history of readers of scripture. My work in Africa had these small beginnings on Egret Point.

My active day is now ordered toward worldwide ministries, especially with university students in Africa—all from this tiny Point.

This is not a lonely venue, but a place of lively active solitude, rich in companionship, with the fellowship of the saints, and with the Giver of life.

Why?

Why have I chosen free and active solitude? The simple answer is that few could tolerate living with me with my canyons of books and introverted ways—no one, that is, except she who actually did it, who braved my idiosyncrasies for more than four decades before malignant cells invaded her lovely flesh.

Following decades of active teaching, partnering, parenting, and constant motion, I yearned for solitude. Why? I had already lived a full life as lover, father, professor, and writer. Now, having lost her to cancer, I was alone. I found I was, as Cole Porter wrote, a "one-gal guy." Crosby sang it in *High Society*.

This is not a plea for pity or a silent claim to wisdom or righteousness, but simply a hard fact of life: my loss, and my desire to grow through it. I wanted to learn to live without her since with her was no option. I prayed for grace as I turned toward a solitary life of prayer, study, and silence that I have single-mindedly pursued since her passing.

I am neither hurried nor hindered at Egret Point. This is now the life to which the Creator has called me after having first called me to marriage, fatherhood, and active family life. Now the still, small voice speaks of an ordered life of prayer, study, and solitude.

Some friends have countered that a more responsible and engaged choice would have been to live a life once again in the mainstream of mating and scrambling, providing and protecting. I knew myself well enough to realize that would be going backward. I have lived that life. I have been married. I have fathered and raised beautiful children with my endearing companion. The union with her is incomparable, irrevocable, and now complete and without regret. It does not need another substitute or period of extension. Now, years later, I am aware of her presence day by day.

I have been called into this quiet place for this new life. I am grateful. Within these wide boundaries I am thankful for my immediate family living nearby around these places where I grew up. They have given me a rich bonding with those who love me.

This is just background for the awaiting story, which is an inward journey to the center of my heart. I invite you to join. It is time to introduce the characters of this little story.

The Characters: You, Her, Me

You

In these meditations I am in a conversation with you, Lord, and with her — my late companion of forty-six years who is still ever on my mind, and with myself. It is a collection of thank-you notes to you about you, her, and me.

There are only three characters that hang out much around Egret Point: you (God), her (my life partner), and me. We are not equal. God is God. She is gone. I am still alive to tell about it.

Wherever the uncapitalized word *you* occurs, it points to God. I beg the reader to give me this temporary license: when I speak of *you* I am not addressing any other living person, but only the One worthy of worship. *You* means the divine Thou, the One who reads closely the thoughts of the reader of this book. *You* means the divine knower of our motivations and conscience, that singular Thou who is the source and end of all things. Not me, not her, not the reader. The reader is dropping in upon a quiet conversation between you, her, and me.

None of these meditations is addressed first to human readers, all to God. Unconditional adoration addressed to anyone other than God is called idolatry.

The cast is small (you, her, and me), but all the characters are real. Meanwhile, whoever happens in upon this conversation is completely welcome.

Her

But what about *her*, my irreplaceable companion in love and family? Let Emily Dickinson speak of her for whom few words are appropriate:

The soul selects her own society,
Then shuts the door;
On her divine majority
Obtrude no more.

Unmoved, she notes the chariot's pausing
At her low gate;
Unmoved, an emperor is kneeling
Upon her mat.

I've known her from an ample nation
Choose one;
Then close the valves of her attention
Like stone.

She choose just one. Which one? I am the one she chose.

But why speak of her in a generic sense? No woman I know can be generic. Each one is uniquely that one.

Step aside for a moment. Listen to the timbre of my voice. It changes when I speak of her. If I took you aside to speak descriptively of her, I would be almost whispering to you — words like *stunning, brilliant, spontaneous, funny, graceful, appealing*. But in relation to her, her reality, all these words are pitifully thin. Only the tiny sigh that follows such words reveals her uniqueness.

Everyone loved her, and not a few fell in love with her. She was an actress when I met her, and I as awkward as Mr. Chips. If you were looking for a recognizable public visual image of her you might think of an intriguing face like Audrey Hepburn or inward depth of subtle self-awareness like Liv Ullmann, or always elegant movement like Ginger Rogers. The *her* I am failing to describe had immeasurable vitality, quickness, intuitive depth, honesty, candor.

Yet compared to the pleasure of being the mother of our children and my life partner, all these descriptions faded into background. She waved it off as not worth mentioning when I let others know (only rarely) that during the early years of our marriage she was a brilliant performer, director, and actress. She regarded it as insignificant that she once played opposite David Niven.

There are many references to her in these meditations, revealing how often she is on my mind, in my prayers, as if now by my side. Though she is physically away, she is found often unexpectedly on the Point. The healing that has taken place here since her passing has made my life seem more complete now than at any time since she was alive to bless each day.

Me

Me? The one she chose. The unique person to whom I point when I say "I." I still ponder what I mean by "I" apart from her.

The voice you hear is that of an awkward teacher of university students who is illuminating as much of his own inner life as fragile words can contain. As a lover, husband, and father, a winner in life but loser of the most loved, I am a sufferer of the normal wounds of finitude—enough to convey a glimpse of life's wholeness.

Surrounding these characters at a wider and more obscured angle are a vast chorus of those we together most loved. They extended around the world and time to a beloved community stretching from now to eternity. They include specific living historic communities of present-day classic Christian believers living out of a historic community of faith. They reach back to a living community that encompasses the prophets who anticipated the incarnation in the form of promise, the apostles and martyrs who attested it with their blood, and the teachers of sacred texts who understood all of these together. *We* means implicitly those whose hearts are already turned to God.

An Ancient Way of Living in Time

Just as the day moves from phase to phase, so does the cycle of meditation proceed through time, by tones as different as light and dark.

The sevenfold cycle of meditation is best grasped by active participation. Walking through the hours is different from reading about them.

The meaning of the meditative cycle becomes clearer only through taking these steps many times, enough that the rhythm of walking flows smoothly. Then it becomes easier to discern the seven very different "hours." Each one has its own emotive mood. Each is expressed in different images and metaphors and scriptural references in the daily seasons of prayer. They weave together the Psalms so as to illumine the mystery of the story of salvation, the meaning of history.

A walking journey requires taking steps. No one person can walk for another. To carry a toddler is not to let the toddler walk. The walk I make is not the walk the reader will make, though it will have some similar contours and analogies.

Meditations in this collection are intensely personal. They are not editorial opinions. They may not be directly applicable to another person's circumstances.

They are offered as a bundle of images that taste the scent of each period of the cycle of prayer. They offer snapshots made in striking moments of light and shade. They hope to make the hours of life with God more rich and deep. To come alive, they are not only read or spoken but walked through in time.

In Any Hue of Light or Darkness

The purpose of these meditations is to make it easier to praise God, enjoy God, be with God. Anytime. In any hue of light or darkness. The structure of time we can learn from the canonical hours is a time-tested frame.

God is forever reaching downward for us to assist us in reaching upward toward God.

Whatever level of one's time commitment, these meditations hope to make this passageway easier, more natural, more accessible. The point is to wisely order the priceless time we are given to sanctify the whole of time.

Each glimpse points straightaway to some particular event of daily life through light and shadow. Each one sees the changing shades of reality set in one of seven phases of the daily cycle we all experience.

Seven Blessings a Day

A defining text for the hours comes from the Italian saint Benedict of Nursia, beginning with the psalm:

"Seven times a day I have given praise to you," said the psalmist. This sacred number is fulfilled by the faithful daily in order to perform the responsibilities of our service at these set apart times: lauds, prime, terce, sext, none, vespers, and compline, beginning from the predawn hour to the first, then third, sixth, ninth, and twelfth hour until midnight. It was of these hours that the psalmist spoke of seven times a day. In these times we offer daily praise to our Creator for the judgments of His justice and rise at night also to praise him.

Benedict, Rule, 16

This sequence of meditations leaves each reader to define the timeframe in accord with each one's actual circumstances. It can be a seven-period day, or a seven-day week, or seven weeks, or any comparable timeframe. It can be translated into the frame of the seven seasons of the Christian year: Advent, Christmas, Epiphany, Lent, Easter, Pentecost, and Trinity. It could be undertaken during a crisis or in quiet times.

The Hours Defined

An *hour* here refers not to sixty minutes but to the phases of the spiritual and light cycle of the day.

The canonical hours are a series of acts and services of personal and common prayer to be privately prayed or commonly sung at regular times of the day to put the mind in touch with the Psalms of scripture, the songs of ancient Israel.

The specific feature of a particular canonical hour hinges on its time of light or darkness and its relation to labor and rest. The hour responds to a universal human need to praise, confess, and dedicate that arises from the particular requirements of that time of day. The Psalms of sacred scripture speak the Word of God, revealing the divine intention and fitting prayer for that hour.

Through these periods of prayer, or set-aside hours (even if they last only minutes by clock time), believers intend to sanctify the whole of time, through day and night, both in inactive rest and in active vocation. These periods serve as timely ways of ordering the sanctity of the whole of life, not just parts of it.

The meditations of this journey arise out of the patterns of prayer of the canonical hours. All things finite are ordered in time. Early Christianity structured daily life around timely prayers that focus on a spiritual purpose pertinent to that particular time of day.

Scripture through the Hours

The background of each meditation comes from the story of salvation indicated in psalm or scripture for that time of day or season of grace. The scripture text presents an episode or glimpse of the history of salvation that bears upon the hour, a word from the Lord on the particular theme pertinent to that time. The scripture texts focus and intensify meditation on the divine revelation at that time of day. In the mid-morning (at Terce, the third hour of daylight), for example, there is a recollection of the descent of the Holy Spirit, praying for God's Spirit to pour down grace upon the active life of the believer in his daily vocation.

These times have been modified by many traditions, from Coptic to Benedictine, from Eastern to Western, from Reformation to modern. They are not unalterably standardized. The pattern found here is on the whole the most common or consensual tradition.

Thus in regular brief times of prayer (from a minute to a quarter hour) at roughly three-hour intervals the whole twenty-four hour day is pervaded with these seven oases of prayer. Among Protestants (especially of the Lutheran, Reformed, Anglican, and Wesleyan traditions) this pattern often became simplified as morning prayer and evening prayer, or Lauds and Vespers, whether prayed in community or family devotions or individually. Contemporary believers who in some form observe regular morning and evening prayers are touching the heart of the ancient pattern.

Implicitly the whole day of prayer is crystallized in the coming and going and return of light into the world. The One who fully embodies the Light of the World is identified in the New Testament. The believer's life is constantly illumined by his light.

As Christmas and Easter anchor the Christian year, so do Lauds and Vespers anchor the hours in the daily life of prayer from beginning of light to end. They introduce and conclude the day's activity in the celebration of God's holiness.

The Rising and Setting of the Sun

In the history of religions, rites emerge out of actual challenging events in human life: birth, initiation, marriage, sickness, and death. They arise out of particularly significant moments of natural change: the cycle of seasons and the rising and setting of the sun.

It is hard for modern people with artificial light to understand just how important the night-and-day cycle was to those who lived before modern technology. Each new dawn brought new life. Each sunset brought to a virtual halt all the usual working activities made possible by daylight. We sense a bit of that awe during a total blackout, when the customary artificial light and electricity is suddenly absent. Then we grasp how much we have taken for granted the gifts of light and energy.

The celebration of the rising and setting of the sun is found in every known human culture. Rites throughout human history have celebrated the new day and prepared the community and family for the night. Each new day rehearses a new beginning. Each night is given over to vigilance on the part of protectors and trustful rest on the part of others. Praise is typically offered at day's beginning and confession at day's end.

Like their neighboring cultures, the ancient Hebrews provided ample evidences of their daily pattern of morning and evening prayer. Unlike their neighbors, however, these prayers were based on a strictly monotheistic premise: the one and only God is the giver of all time, both night and day. That one is revealed in history, for Jews in the expectation of the Messiah, for Christians in the fulfillment of that expectation.

When Jesus came to personally incarnate the true God in time, these Hebraic patterns were reshaped into a transformed awareness of the sanctification of time seen in the light of God's own coming in person. Christianity did not simply repeat the Jewish tradition, but received it and modified it into the classic Christian understanding of daily time.

God and Time

God has plenty of time. It is finite humans who run short. In this way God teaches us about time. Each being in time is wise to receive time patiently in relation to its incomparably patient Giver and its end.

It may take time before a lost postal letter is discovered and sent to that single individual for whom it is intended. That one will know instantly what it means. The time in between does not alter the message. It becomes significant when it is heard.

Each scene recorded here takes less than a minute to grasp. For those prudent about their time, this journey minimally calls for only seven minutes a day. Let it be wisely distributed over a few weeks of spiritual formation. This may be a better investment of time than a straight-through read.

It does not necessarily take large amounts of time to sanctify the whole cycle of time. It does not require a church building or a monastic setting or a celibate life or a snow peak or a desert in order to participate, though these may for some be constructive or helpful. Time for these meditations can be any length.

Now

The eternal moment cannot be measured in clock time because it transcends clock time. *Now* embraces every time. What we call "now" is entering history as eternal Word every moment. Christians view this moment under the analogy of the incarnation.

Life with God is lived out in ordinary time. Since we have bodies, the process is enfleshed in us by grace. It embraces the concrete situation viewed within the eternal Word.

Even a moment of concentrated meditation can place this unique "now" in touch with the eternal, who is always now. The Lord invites: "Ask and you shall receive." Any can pray for grace. Those who pray for grace to sanctify the whole of their time have taken the first step.

The traditional services of the Book of Hours normally require only a few minutes. These pages do not repeat the traditional services but prize and presuppose the tradition underlying them. Texts of these prayers and readings are widely available.

In the ancient texts of the Book of Hours, all normally hear a psalm and some other scripture readings (at least one from the Old and one from the New Testament) and hymns and prayers fitting to that phase of the cycle of the day. In some traditions you will hear added readings from the ancient Christian writers or the lives of the saints.

Learning More on the Hours

Where can you go to learn more about praying through the hours? Seek out a spiritual advisor or soul guide. Or go directly to the classic books of liturgy in all classic Christian traditions.

The rhythm and language of the hours can be learned independently at one's own pace. They may also be learned online. Anyone can retrieve daily prayers from any number of websites, whether Orthodox, Catholic, Coptic, Anglican, or Protestant: www.ocf.org/OrthodoxPage/prayers; www.catholic.org/clife/prayers; www.Agpeya.org; http://scriptorium.lib.duke.edu.

You may choose from many versions of the Liturgy of the Hours. You can borrow a Breviary or Liturgy of the Hours from a library or church. Among the easiest to use is Maxwell E. Johnson's *Benedictine Daily Prayer* (Collegeville, Minn.: Liturgical Press, 2005).

Thomas Oden, completed on the Feast Day
of St. Crispina of Numidia († 304 AD)

PART 1

Book I: Soulprints

Thematic Focus: *Finding Myself without Her*

Learning the Gracious Life: *Common Grace*

Cycle of the First Fortnight
First Week
Second Week

First Week

DAY 1

Before Dawn (Vigils)

my soul is quiet

> the fish are swimming in the hidden caverns of the night
> the starlings are settled in the trees
> the light is gone
> the leaves are still
> my soul is quiet

First Hour of Morning (Lauds)

one is enough

> one is enough
> one life
> one love
> one eternal now
> even one day contains all of these
> even one hour contains more than all of these

Mid-morning — Third Hour (Terce)

listen to the rain

> listen to the sound of rain
> the crash of wind and wave
> the earth receiving life
> the heavens giving life
>
> while the sun is hidden
> the thirsty seeds are being drenched with living days

Noon — Sixth Hour (Sext)

an eternity waiting for a time

> this slender space is an eternity waiting for a time to happen
> this colored sky has been so long preparing
> made possible by millions of moments preceding
> each never repeated
>
> only slow unnamed utterances ring out from my heart

Mid-afternoon — Ninth Hour (None)

by water's edge

> close by the water's edge my soul is filled
> standing silent like the great white egret
> gently balanced as if on the verge
> with ruffled feathers in the wind
>
> here I have come to live
> to breathe under the deep shade
> of the high archway of summer leaves
> shielded from the burning prairie sun
> in quest of little more than a brook and a breeze
>
> I need no other bliss
> no fitful urge for someone else to see what I now see
> no restless craving for another's eye
> no obsessive need for company
>
> except for her
> with whom I will rise again on the last day

Evensong (Vespers)

reaching for you

> let the highest branches of the pines reach for you
> let each uplifted stem draw warmth
> from the last remaining rays of sun
> let deep roots gain nourishment from the cool day

each living cell prepare for coming winter
let the pipevine swallowtails praise you with blue and golden
      wings
let each changing pattern of light on water refract your glory

refine my thoughts
sharpen my discernment
embolden my courage
lift me up to you, Lord
let me share in your glory
where she now abides

Nighttime (Compline)

the exhaling day

descending slow
suddenly gone
the sun has visited the day
now leaving only the flowered remnants of a colored sky
only the breath of an exhaling sky

may my time tomorrow be spent
as you have spent today with me
offering light and warmth
to the just and unjust alike

I rest easy with her memory on my pillow

Interlude: Life with God in Time

The hours of prayer are a calming feature of the Christian life, a tested way of ordering time. This life is like a journey through time.

The daily warfare of the Christian life is like an athletic contest, an adventurous life of discipline, a rigorous challenge. Then it becomes unexpectedly a celebration, a feast.

Sometimes the day is like a journey through a desert, when an oasis means life or death. Then suddenly the willowed spring offers refreshing shade.

These are quiet meditations, interspersed with a series of interludes on how the day may be filled with prayer in accord with ancient Christian believers' habits.

What Is Meant by an "Hour"

Believers in both Jewish and Christian traditions practiced a special way of ordering time called "praying through the hours." An "hour" is not a literal hour but a slice of experience flowing through each cast of light. Each "hour" was a set-aside time of prayer. The Psalms fueled the acts of prayer in each phase of the day. The sojourners memorized the Psalms, and pondered them daily at planned times.

They found that the life of the believer takes shape within an order of daily events that unfold through seasons of darkness and light. This stream flows through the hours of the Christian community at prayer. From early times they were called canonical hours. A canon is a rule. *Canonical* means by an ordered channel of canon law, of the discipline of believers, of church practice.

DAY 2

Before Dawn (Vigils)

prayer for a contrite heart

> I stumble in the night
> reaching for something to hold me upright
> clutching for a foothold in time
> accountable to choices I have made
> even when I hardly knew I made them
>
> O source and end of days
> from whom my freedom draws every breath
> toward whom all my acts of preference finally tend
> eternal maker of time

I cannot plead ignorance in your presence
nor ask for any gift but a contrite heart

First Hour of Morning (Lauds)

light and shadow

you give light and shadow
to a thin and restive world
you give depth and space
to here and now
a rock to shelter the wandering traveler

you who are light incomparable
give now new quietness to the dawn

above all give yourself
who come in person to human history
as love enfleshed
come now to my quiet place
knock gently on my door
teach me to welcome you

as she welcomed me

Mid-morning — Third Hour (Terce)

a wild ribbon

shape me this day as a song
a dart to be thrown
a wild ribbon of gratitude
as a cork tossing on high waves

Noon — Sixth Hour (Sext)

the architecture of an endive leaf

the intricate design of a purple endive leaf
stuns and fills the eye
evocative, ingenious, meant to be
spun from incalculably complex vectors of forces
hidden in glacial physics

yet taking present form in only one time and place
energies working silently though countless winters
have shaped the disposition of this garden leaf
won through testing in specific places
where seeds have fallen
where shoots have grown through drought and storm

a human gardener's hand has been at work
along with you
without whose hand no hand would be

Mid-afternoon — Ninth Hour (None)

the remedy of slow silence

there is a remedy found in slow silence
borne of unhurried breathing from the center

but when the mind moves too fast to track
it is robbed of memory
even while floating in a swirling sea of memory fragments
spinning ever faster
bewildered by the rising flood of possibilities

slow me down for memory's sake
when I have thoughts I cannot think a moment later
since captive to the falling flow
speeding at breakneck pace
where no one has time to stop and remember
what the third prior move was
unlike chess where memory makes all the difference

I keep her in my heart

Evensong (Vespers)

the nesting of the snowy egret

the dark valley is blessed nightly
by the visitation of these great white birds
awakening in me the thought of her
as if she were here

though now at a distance too far to touch
yet I savor the simple beauty of her imagined presence

you, love, who were ever self-effacing
dwell in a radiant light above
in the stunning transparency of your soul

you dwell in a lofty place gleaming in the evening sun
refracted in the pastels of rippling waters

I am coming

Nighttime (Compline)

let doors be closed

let doors be closed on evening's light
let the flesh of sleeping children curl into a ball
let lights be dimmed
let sounds of evening take possession of the night

for now I've done enough of good or ill
my budget spent

a sliver of unsullied light hints toward another day
tomorrow will return from the east
to birth its unknown possibilities

Interlude: The Bells of the Hours

The bells that announced these hours provided the meditative life of a village with a practiced way of consecrating the whole day to God. They invited the whole arena of mundane life to reflect God's own holiness and justice, even if briefly.

Praying is less a duty than a gift. The food is offered for savoring, not wolfing. Believers find that the gift of prayer is not incidental. It is vital for living a healthy life. Its patterns are certified by centuries of experience. They have weathered all seasons. They serve as a framework into which the whole life of prayer may find repose.

Life in the Spirit is intrinsically a flow with time, moving at its own pace through its own distinct phases of light and shadow. The benefit of praying the hours deepens as we experience them and test them through the full circle of darkness and light, night and day in steady recurrence. The Book of Hours offers companionship on a long, every-day journey.

Ringing the Bells

In Roman and Byzantine times, the bell in the center of the town rang out before dawn to awaken (vigils), at the beginning of the working day at six o'clock in the morning (prime, the "first hour"). It struck again at about nine o'clock in the morning (terce, the "third hour"), and tolled again for the midday break at noon (sext, the "sixth hour"), then signaled the middle of the afternoon at about three o'clock (none, the "ninth hour"), and rang to close the work day at about sunset (the time for evening vespers), and finally to welcome the night (compline). These hours corresponded roughly with the times of prayer that had been provided in Israel at the time of the writing of Psalm 119:164, "Seven times a day I praise you."

These "hours" ordered and united the day not only for the worshiping communities but for the secular city, the society. Church bells would ring out to remind those within hearing distance about which prayers were being sung by the gathered community for the scattered community. Those who could do so would participate in the prayers wherever they were, whatever they were doing, in whatever ways feasible. This elicited a wider spiritual community that symbolically united all who had ears to hear. The city of man became for a time a mirror of the city of God.

Thus in the traditional Christian ordering of daytime there is every three daylight hours a pause from work for prayer, at 6:00, 9:00 a.m., and 12:00 noon, and after noon at 3:00, 6:00, 9:00 p.m., and then 12:00 at night (variable in different traditions). These times formed the scaffold around which the biblical cycle of a whole night and day was structured. The challenge of spiritual formation was to learn to live the whole day in God's presence every day.

Life with God is intended to flow through every moment of every day, including work and rest. The full day of sleeping, working, and persevering is fittingly punctuated by deliberate set-aside times to pray and hear the written Word in order that the whole day may be sanctified. So it was in the earliest Christian centuries that these patterns developed from early morning to late evening, interspersed approximately every three hours. Daily work was blended together with prayer and scripture, ordered to make the whole day an integral response to God's presence.

Jesus said: "Therefore keep watch because you do not know when the owner of the house will come back — whether in the evening, or at midnight, or when the rooster crows, or at dawn" (Mark 13:35). Be ready for his coming at any time of the day or night.

It is fitting to praise him all through the day and night. I cannot be ready for his coming today if I do not remain attentive in each phase of the day.

The Biblical Pattern of the Daily Hours

This pattern of daily prayer grew out of the Old Testament practice of reciting psalms and prayers at seven set times of the day. Psalm 119:164–65 states:

> Seven times a day I praise you
> for your righteous laws.
> Great peace have they who love your law,
> And nothing can make them stumble.

Why seven times? As many days as it took the Lord to make the world and rest following creation, so many are the set-apart times of welcoming God in the ordinary day. As six are times of work, one is a time of rest. The receptive seventh "hour" perfects and completes the other active round of six. In these pages we extend this pattern to embrace seven weeks, the timeframe for the whole cycle of mediations, hence seven weeks of seven days each with seven hours — in total 343 meditations — are all based on the pattern of God's work in the world from its beginning.

These seven times of Jewish psalmody became the basis for the Christian version of the Hebraic order of daily prayer as it became clarified in the light of the incarnation and resurrection of Christ in the New Testament.

This pattern was passed down through the centuries from the apostles to early Christians. By the time of Hippolytus († 236 AD) we see a growing development of the canonical hours or ordered hours of prayer. From the earliest Christian decades there have been Christian believers who followed the psalmists and apostles in this sevenfold pattern of daily meditation. For two thousand years the series of hours of daily prayer has been a regular daily practice of many Jews and Christians.

These times of prayer were ordered in relation to powerful texts of scripture as they pertain to experienced moments of the day and night. From the earliest days of Jewish and Christian piety, these hours have been oriented around meditating on psalms and scripture, singing hymns, and asking for the Spirit's guidance. The intent is to "set apart" or sanctify the particular periods of the day in order to offer up the whole day to life with God.

Every child learns that clocks have twelve hours and not twenty-four. But why? The practice of numbering twelve hours between sunrise and sunset comes from the ancient Jewish and Christian practice of distinguishing between hours of night (nocturnal hours) and hours of day (diurnal). When the eleventh-century Benedictine monks made the first mechanical clocks, they were distinguishing the night hours of intercession from the day hours. Out of twenty-four hours in the secular day, seven of these were "set aside" canonically.

Now, back to the journey.

——————————————— **DAY 3** ———————————————

Before Dawn (Vigils)

singing through the night

> the distant light that dances on a dark breeze
> touching caps of chilly waters
> glinting and breathing throughout the night
> however weak its random blink
> serves the restless surf
> to picture morning

tracing the day now done
rehearsing for the day not yet
recalling the opulent afterglow of the plump sun

let that fragile light bestow hope on all the hushed creatures of
        the night
let it be a beacon of patience to the imprisoned
attesting the source of light in time
let it flicker calm above uneasy waters
singing through the black wind
a song I sang with her

First Hour of Morning (Lauds)

beyond being old

you are the oldest of the old
beyond being old
since you were even ancient
before old began
yet still you sweeten any taste of time

I too am a bit old
seen from the narrow angles of these times
though in relation to you just born

Mid-morning—Third Hour (Terce)

glimpses into the soul

all I get are glimpses
not still portraits
not legal papers
not verifiable news reports
not hammered words on tables of stone
into my soul
all I get are glimpses

Noon — Sixth Hour (Sext)

each task its time

> each duty waits its turn
> the tasks pile up and jam upstream
> each task has its time
>
> with no tasks left at the end of the day

Mid-afternoon — Ninth Hour (None)

the mystery in which I bathe

> the heady smell of burnt cedar fills the air
> crepe myrtle offers fragrance to the cove
> while I cling to a fading sky
>
> you fire the veiled synapses of my brain
> you welcome me to the unfathomable mystery in which I bathe
> in which I am finding out who I am
>
> still graced by her presence even when away

Evensong (Vespers)

quiet my soul

> settle me now into slow time's remedies
> uplift my spirit
> that I may hear your voice through distant thunder
> behold your glory in the dying evening
> that I may find my way back to who I am before you
>
> so let the world go by for now
> let it pass
> that your own eternal word be spoken
> in closing moments of the day

Nighttime (Compline)

listen through the shadows

> just this moment I need
> only this now

to listen through the shadows
to hear you

grant peace amid soft shades of fading light
stretching the shadows into the deepening greens of the high
        trees
beside the unhurried surface of the stream
where she came softly without hurrying

DAY 4

Before Dawn (Vigils)

the bill is due

    the price paid for deception is dear
    it never stops asking for payment
    its odor lingers heavy on the soul
    the bill is due

First Hour of Morning (Lauds)

the web

    a delicate glistening web is suspended
    over the limp reaches of a willow
    holding fast against the wind

    it overwhelms clumsy words
    to describe its glowing silhouette
    its brilliance in the sun
    its practical function for sustaining fragile life
    the result of millennia of practice by tiny creatures seeking food
    to live another day

Mid-morning—Third Hour (Terce)

as I flee the city

    the decaying city is ever under construction
    with mortar set to bricks then thrown away
    as if forever to be built yet always unfinished
    forever tending toward ruin

let me flee the city for the garden
where bees rule and apples weep
let me breathe the sunlit garden air
where blackbird legions flock to search for seed

Noon — Sixth Hour (Sext)

seeding another life

when winter comes the seeds ride the wind
to seek new soil
yielding to be blown away
to spawn another life
in a place not known before

so you carry me down the stream
to seed and bloom another season
to taste the loam of another landscape
to root in a different clime

now let me yield
to take nimble wing on wind and wave

Mid-afternoon — Ninth Hour (None)

remembering her

ten years ago today she passed
now I pass her picture to a stranger and say inwardly
what a gift
still blessed by her

Evensong (Vespers)

unlike any other

in a secluded cove of a lost lake on a vast plain
amid a thousand scrub oaks and blooming Indian
    blankets
wild flowers of riotous shapes and colors
each one its own distinctive signature
no creature exactly like any other

here I live
in a haven from impediments
where social differences make no difference

here it is easy to see
how magnificent is each tiny instance of your creation
dimly refracting your greater magnificence
who are yourself insurmountably unlike any other

Nighttime (Compline)

nothing yet to grieve

with a sharp pain in my chest I wonder
whether I will be here tomorrow
I do not know but this I know
I have been given every grace already to have a fulfilled life

nothing still to miss
nothing yet to grieve
nothing unresolved
nothing of importance left unsaid

so I speak back to Zarathustra
if asked to live my same life over and over
in eternal recurrence
I say yes quickly without a stutter
a decision I alone can make for me

so often reconfirmed
I walk full blessed through finite time
grateful for the life you've tendered me
willing to face its tragic limits again
again
again

Interlude: Clock Hours and the Canonical Hours

The invention of the basic idea of a clock is ascribed to an Italian clergyman, Ireneo Pacifico, Archdeacon of Verona (778–846), who wrote a poem in Latin called *Argumentum Horologi*. It describes the clock's construction as an imitation of the celestial sphere that rotates in an arc of hours. This poetic work conceptually anticipates the development of more complicated actual mechanisms.

The Rule of Benedict called for a way of ordering time that could offer the fullest possibilities for life with God. The invention of the clock came out of this community of prayer. They had need of an accurate time-ordering norm. To accomplish this ordering of time they were inventive. They tried hourglasses, sand glasses, water clocks, and segmented candle clocks.

Remarkably, the science and art of mechanical clock-making was born within these monastic orders. They were searching for a reliable way to measure the hours. They did not refer to the twenty-four we know, but the seven canonical hours, which is our subject now. The clock was invented to solve the problem of waking up the brother whose task was to ring the carillon to call the community to prayer.

The liturgy of the hours called for prayer seven times a day at specific shades of light and darkness. The clock was invented by spiritual guides to serve a holy purpose: to order work and prayer through day and night, through all tones and traces of vividness and obscurity.

The first modern mechanical clock was a device driven by falling weights with a wheel. It was invented by a Benedictine monk named Gerbert, who later became the bishop of Rome, Silvester II. The breakthrough was the verge escapement, an oscillating gear system that allowed a slowly descending weight on a cord to drive the clockwork at a steady and reliable rate. To this was later added a more precise iron escapement and a crown wheel with teeth that regulated chimes.

By about 1200 AD the Benedictine monks had perfected the basic mechanism of the escapement with its bell-ringing device. It should not surprise us that the first mechanical clock was born in a sanctuary of Christian prayer where the ordered hours were of central importance to maximizing the potential of the life of prayer.

With that ingenious discovery, the concept of a "clockhour" was inaugurated. It became a fixed unit rather than a flexible time. It was always the same, day and night, winter and summer, regardless of the solar and lunar cycles or weather. Cultural historian Lewis Mumford viewed the mechanical clock as the initiating machine of the industrial age. The precision of these clocks is regarded by science historian Donald Cardwell as "the greatest single human invention since that of the wheel."

The Chronicle of Jocelyn of Brakeland (1198 AD) at St. Edmondsbury described a water-driven alarm clock the praying brothers and sisters used to announce early morning matins. Water clocks had been invented before the monastic period, but they were greatly improved and fine-tuned by the monks. With their invention of the mechanical clock, the monks became the first humans to devise a system of telling time mechanically in a way that did not depend upon the direct observance of the cycle of nature.

It all harked back to their seriousness about the regulated hours of prayer according to the psalmist's seven time periods. By 1400, fairly accurate mechanical clock hours had replaced the older Roman and Arabic ways of reckoning time. The clock then came to dominate civic life. It was proudly mounted in public squares. In this way, the canonical hours of the church became transmuted into the profane hours of civic life and set the stage for our modern date books and calendars. For those who want to know more, G. Dohrn-van Rossum wrote the *History of the Hour: Clocks and Modern Temporal Orders* (Chicago: University of Chicago Press, 1996).

———— DAY 5 ————

Before Dawn (Vigils)

viaticum

> wishing I could comfort her now
> sing her to sleep
> make bright her passage
> make fragrant her journey
>
> my prayer reaches out for her
> rests with her
> flows toward her
> as hers did for me
>
> I want to cradle her in peaceful sleep
> to sound a chord to ease her anguish
> delight her dream
> welcome her to tomorrow

First Hour of Morning (Lauds)

all that is

> all that is
> shouts life to time
>
> all that shall be
> glimmers in anticipation of the light of day
>
> all that ever was
> echoes your eternal speech
>
> all that is
> comes alive through your breath
>
> all that shall be
> joins a chorus that never ends
>
> all that was
> bears your fruit now
> remembering your mercy risen with the dying Lord of glory

all that most completely is
penetrates the heart of all that was and ever shall be

Mid-morning—Third Hour (Terce)

the perils surrounding me

a hint of sadness floods the corner of my eye
as I survey the army of ambiguities surrounding me
perils without number

so let quiet and steady labor gradually drain away
the fretfulness of this morning

Noon—Sixth Hour (Sext)

full table

you have brought me to this full table
showered me with undeserved mercy
revealed a vision of your glory
tamed my wayward obsessions
swept over my soul with grace
offered your fullness
given me utterance heart to heart
in words never before heard

you stamp your image upon conscience
provide all I've ever needed
to be myself within the whole

the complete order of the life you've given
rings out from the heights of mountain peaks
to the seas in their lowliness

Mid-afternoon—Ninth Hour (None)

drifting cottonwood seeds

the cottonwoods spread their semen on the dry plains
wasting it on the breeze
except for that one seed that finds its chosen place

blessed by soil and water and weather and time
in precisely the right proportion, blend, and sequence

your mathematics seems so inexact Lord
yet with dazzling outcomes

Evensong (Vespers)

journey to the desert

light of the world
all lights in time are but mirrored glimpses of your light
made known in the history of your coming in the flesh
sung through times of costly anguish
echoing to the last hour of the last day

Nighttime (Compline)

a glimpse of distant fire

the evening's first star gleams
through eons of light years
whispering from far beyond what's called afar
it seems so tiny to the eye
yet reaches over cosmic voids of countless galaxies

visit me from far beyond afar tonight
you who are the light of light
allowing the remote star to refract your radiance

you who are most near
afire with holy love

the star mirrors you
seated high
while bowing low in the vast universe
glowing all day long though obscured in the sun's
         brightness
till night descends

how odd
it takes darkness to see the light so far away

that from unimaginable aloofness
the more earth darkens the brighter starlight yields

when we lift up hands in awe
let them reach up to your immense height
infinitely higher than this tiny glimpse of distant fire

―――――――――――――― **DAY 6** ――――――――――――

Before Dawn (Vigils)

when shadows disappear

> light has softly withdrawn
> from this spinning world
> completely covering all that is
> with its absence

> not that light has ceased
> but calls on other places now
> with illuminating grace

> when shadows disappear in total darkness
> leaving no distinction between light and light
> obscurity rules with all the rights of sovereign night
> to make way for sleep

First Hour of Morning (Lauds)

you gave her life to give to me

> you who first gave me life
> first gave her life
> to give life anew to me
> by your grace she nurtured me to courage
> tutored my slow mind
> she worked through you and you through her

> now look deep into my heart as you would a child
> show me how to speak the simplest words
> draw pictures for me
> make gestures

form sentences
hold out your hand for my first steps

so permit my freedom to play
within the firm constraints of time
that I may grow up whole

Mid-morning—Third Hour (Terce)

suddenly the geese appear

the geese circling high above
make swift appearance
coming in from distant frozen ice
homing in on the sheltered lake

there must be twenty of them
I watch where they select a spot to land
raucously making their entrance known
each with a fit place in the order of arrival

nearby another dozen are touching down
clamorous and splashy
together beautiful and awkward as they slap the water
spattering and spraying
greeting each other's triumph
tussling noisily over proper rank and space

now all are settling down
territorial boundaries established
the newly arrived visitors gather in their cluster
now in a stately parade moving upstream
slow and gracefully
unlike their awkward waddling on shore

here on this remote pond
they know they have nothing to fear
they can safely overnight here
welcomed by the trees

I too feel welcomed by these trees

in this friendly valley

if I were a wide-winged bird flying in from the distant cold
I too would trust this canopy of trees

Noon — Sixth Hour (Sext)

the rhythm of the hours

close at hand to the wisdom of the saints
through the hours the faithful pray
joined with generations of living communion
always in touch even while far apart
among the cloud of witnesses
whose lives are clothed in the radiant garment of the Son

these daily hours pass by
let each soul walk quietly in the Way
living in God

by midday we are learning limits
once more beholding each moment as a gift
within which anything can happen
without whom nothing

Mid-afternoon — Ninth Hour (None)

the tree and its beholder

nature cannot explain itself without reasoned human
        speech
reason cannot speak without human tongue

the blooming pear extends its branches near my window
each leaf blesses its unique space with its singular presence
in touch with its quiet hidden roots

by fall its raiment will be changed entirely

the bloom and fruit depend on my eyes and tongue for a
        description
though they care nothing about any explanation
only air, earth, fire, and water

a tree needs no speech added to be a tree

yet you allow me by grace to be the single observer
of this exquisite face of life
gleaming now in soft white

Evensong (Vespers)

the mallards in pairs

the mallards feed around the lake
always bound to each other
she and he so very different
the larger brighter
the smaller plainer
defining themselves in relation to each other
made one through their differences

life on the lake comes in pairs
yet I am only one

for five of seven decades I've fed and walked and slept
as one of two in a blessed pair
out of being paired I've become the father of my children
through whose lives my happiness has bloomed
and reached out into the night

far from alone I am yet one

Nighttime (Compline)

evoking her gentleness

to her I have remained true beyond time
she true to me within time now spent
as true as we could be for half a century

I still cling to her embrace
quake at the treasured softness of her voice
evoke by heart the gentleness of her eyes
the subtle ways her hair would fall
the way she looked straight through my soul

how despite all my wavering she held fast to me
our love now wrapped in an eternity of remembered joy

———————————————— **DAY 7** ————————————————

Before Dawn (Vigils)

govern me

> come comforter
> reshape the awkward course of my life
> rewrite the plot
> refashion the lengthy contour of my days
> keep me away from bitterness
> come to guide me on time's ever-turning path
> according to your wisdom

> you come to visit just at this point of weakness
> now give me centeredness
> boldness in obedience
> lowliness of spirit to rest this night
> reclining in your arms
> held gently in the unfolding economy of your grace

First Hour of Morning (Lauds)

purple sky

> suddenly the high deep sky appears at dawn
> breathing cool impressions
> clad now in royal purple
> drifting into bone gray clouds

> with eyes wide open
> who could possibly be worthy of this sky
> this air, this subtle hue, this time

> it is pure gift

Mid-morning—Third Hour (Terce)

a plea for more time

> a host of muffled voices weep under buried roots
> crying out for more time to change
> asking for another chance
> pleading for a way to recast choices
> always faced with the answer of never
>
> they know the time for change is spent
> the limits firm
> for them I pray for grace beyond deserving

Noon—Sixth Hour (Sext)

to strive and not to strive

> I come before you who called me
> first to strive under the law
> then not to strive under grace
> then again to strive
> as an expression of freedom under grace

Mid-afternoon—Ninth Hour (None)

where saints have stood unafraid

> walk with me through ancient amphitheatres
> where lions ravished lambs
> where saints stood unafraid
>
> let me touch the sand where the faithful bled
> take me to that garden in Carthage
> where Cyprian was beheaded
> the bald hill where Perpetua lies buried
> the oratories where your saints gave witness with their blood
>
> I will pray there with them
> that my spirit be given grace to attest with them your truth
> that new light may appear in these dark dungeons
> that my lips may attest with them

your death on the wasteland tree
your risen life with them now

Evensong (Vespers)

descent into the night

as your incarnate Son descended into the darkness of the
grave
to preach to the spirits in prison
let me descend with him this evening
plummet with trust into the nether world
into the baptismal sea
and then to Abraham's Bosom

Nighttime (Compline)

without a trace

to what realm did this day disappear
so swiftly and without a trace

gone as the heron flies quietly away
absent as the storm on a clear night
yet present as memory and desire

where did this tiny epoch go
a dot on history's page
why did it leave so fast and so completely
without a trace

Second Week

—————————— DAY 1 ——————————

Before Dawn (Vigils)

how darkness teaches the eye

> the eye is made to see the light
> it does not do well in the darkness

> yet dark itself instructs the eye
> teaching the precious value of the light

> darkness spreads a silent backdrop for the coming day
> it takes deep darkness to grasp the beauty of the morning

> in darkest corners the eye most looks for light
> like a weary traveler

> in utter darkness even the slenderest light is prized
> the dungeon captive yearns more for light than food

> even the tiniest slip of light
> allows the eye to dance in hope

> absence of light invites new hope
> except for darkness there would be no star

First Hour of Morning (Lauds)

pray through the hours

> when repentance is misplaced
> piety riddled with pretense
> prayer reduced to grasping
> salvation history thinned down to gouache feelings
> holy teaching diluted into travel talk

> teach us again to pray through the hours you give us
> whether late or early in the day

join us with the beloved community
in humble praise

Mid-morning—Third Hour (Terce)

this vanishing wedge of time

> teach me how to live
> within this vanishing wedge of time
> the moment of your coming
> as troubadour with trumpet
> bearing gifts of frankincense

Noon—Sixth Hour (Sext)

I am free but you more so

> when I say you
> to you who overleap all my broken analogies
> I weep for true speech

> even the analogies from personhood, self and
> > freedom
> do not describe even a scrap of all of who you are
> yet if I do not speak to you personally
> I miss too much of who you are as incomparably free
> as I am free but you more so

> meanwhile the bride awaits your return

Mid-afternoon—Ninth Hour (None)

I plead with the wind

> I plead with the wind
> to take me back to her
> unfurl the sail to catch the wind
> as I bend all thoughts toward her
> moving the fabric against the breeze
> rudder against wave
> yearning for the distant port

she dreams alone in a harbor far away
she whispers to the angels to impel the wind
to power the sail
to give courage to the sailor
who slants all thoughts toward her
longing for his distant destination

Evensong (Vespers)

open up the contrite heart

the cello is finely tuned
the time unhindered
the hour descending toward darkness
the memory full of promptings
the time seasoned to open up the contrite heart
to bow and bare its inward fractures

my soul is ripe for molding

you who are listening
speak

Nighttime (Compline)

the graying down of time

there is no color lingering in the sky
not one fleck left of gold or peach or azure
only grays and blacks remaking a stark horizon

this is where I now recline
by grace in time
where I live now as I turn toward sleep

let waters move gradually on their steady course
at their own pace toward ever lower depths
let night air move where it tends in its own way and time

may my soul flow in tempo with yours
as the breeze moves through silent time

Interlude: The Hours in History

The practice of the cycle of hours did not begin in the middle ages. It had a sustained history from Judaism through the apostles straight on to the early church writers, continuing through and past the Reformation. The most familiar form of the Western hours comes from the 525 AD rule of Benedict. Long before Benedict, however, this pattern had been practiced along the Nile and in the East before, and only then flowed north to Europe.

The roots of the seven hours go all the way back to ancient Jewish practices during the exile. This way of ordering the life of prayer was practiced by Jesus and his disciples. From the apostles it was carried over into the devotion of the early Christian church and continues in an unbroken tradition to our own day.

Praying under the Hebraic Covenant

The Divine Office owes its remote origin to at least as early as the Aaronic priests (c. 1280 BC) who offered a morning and evening sacrifice daily (Ex. 29:38–29). Eventually, these sacrifices moved from the mobile Tabernacle to the established Temple built by Solomon in Jerusalem a millennium before Jesus.

During the Babylonian Exile (587–521 BC), when the first Temple had been destroyed, the first synagogues were established, with the services composed of Torah, psalms, and hymns at fixed hours of the day. In these local synagogues the "sacrifice of praise" began to be observed instead of bloody sacrifices of animals in the Temple.

While in Babylon, the accustomed practice of Daniel in set times of prayer was described: "he went into his house: and opening the windows in his upper chamber towards Jerusalem, he knelt down three times a day, and adored and gave thanks before his God, as he had been accustomed to do before" (Daniel 6:10). These were practiced regularly. Gabriel is reported to have appeared to Daniel in a vision and touched him — when? "About the time of the evening sacrifice" (Daniel 9:21).

After the people returned to Judea, and the Temple was rebuilt, the prayer services that had developed in Babylon for the local assemblies or synagogues of the people were brought into Temple use. In addition to Morning and Evening temple prayer to accompany the sacrifices, there was also a practice of prayer at the Third, Sixth, and Ninth Hours of the day. This became the basis for the order of the later Book of Hours.

The Psalms

The Psalms provide many evidences of a threefold fixed-time practice of prayer: "Evening and morning, and at noon I will speak and declare: and he shall hear my voice" (Psalm 55:17). "I will meditate on thee in the morning"; "I rose at midnight to give praise to thee." "The just man mediates on the law day and night" (Ps. 1:2).

The key text is in Psalm 119:164: "Seven times a day I have given praise to thee, for the judgments of thy justice." This sevenfold pattern of daily prayer was in place in fifth-century BC Judaism. It was transformed into a Christian order of prayer after Christianity proclaimed the fulfillment of the messianic promises of the prophets.

How the Apostles Kept the Hours

In New Testament times Jews prayed the *Shema* (Deut. 6:4–9; 11:13–21; Num. 15:37–41) morning and evening, and other benedictions three times daily. From the very beginnings of Christianity, those who were baptized "devoted themselves to the teaching of the apostles and to the community, to the breaking of the bread, and to prayer" (Acts 2:42). They prayed with one accord. They devoted themselves to prayer at traditionally specified times.

The Acts of the Apostles make it clear that Christians continued to pray at these same hours of late Judaic prayer (third hour as seen in Acts 2:15; sixth hour as seen in Acts 10:9; 10:3, 13). The apostles are also reported as praying at midnight, and on the third, sixth, and ninth hour (Latin *terce, sext, none*: Acts 10:3, 9; 16:25). "About midnight Paul and Silas were praying and singing hymns to God" (16:25). The apostles did not invent it; they observed it as taught by Jewish practice as it was transformed by the history of Jesus.

The prayers that appear in the New Testament refract many of the same elements as the previous Jewish practice: recital or chanting of psalms and reading of the Old Testament. To these were added the writings of the apostles: Gospels, Acts, and Epistles. Biblical hymns and canticles were sung: Gloria in Excelsis, Magnificat, Nunc Dimittis. The apparent complexity of the praying of the hours today makes them seem distant from Jewish prayer, but from there they are derived, by gradual changes as they became transformed by Christian interpretation of Jewish scripture.

Even when the apostles no longer shared in the explicit Temple sacrifices, they enjoyed its fulfillment in the "breaking of the bread" (the Eucharist). Meanwhile they continued to return to the Temple at fixed and customary hours of prayer. In the book of Acts Peter and John visited the Temple for the afternoon prayers at the ninth hour as was their custom (Acts 3:1).

The earliest church made a defining decision prompted by the Spirit: Gentiles are called to be among the community of believers, previously Jewish. This arose from a vision Peter had while praying at noon on a rooftop to observe sixth-hour prayer: "And on the next day, while they were going on their journey and drawing nigh to the city, Peter went up to the higher parts of the house to pray, about the sixth hour." (Acts 10:9). The vision was of a sheet filled with both clean and unclean animals, pointing toward the mission to the Gentiles, to receive all that God had created as clean.

It was not by accident that Peter was on that rooftop at noon. It was an expected act of devotion for any faithful soul, and so for the early Christian apostles. Peter was far away from the Jerusalem temple, but he was keeping the traditionally appointed time of prayer. Later Cornelius reported that he saw in a vision about the ninth hour of the day an angel of God coming to instruct him: "Four days ago, unto this hour, I was praying in my house at the ninth hour and behold a man stood before me in white apparel" (Acts 10:30).

Another report in the book of Acts shows the faithfulness of the apostles to these patterns of prayer: "About midnight Paul and Silas were praying and singing hymns to God, and the other prisoners were listening to them" (Acts 16:25).

The Christian practice of praying through the hours grew from the Jewish practice of reciting psalms and prayers at prescribed times of the day. The Christian community from the outset recited the Psalms as prayers. They became embedded in virtually all their daily prayers (Acts 4:23–30). The reading and memorizing of the Psalms has remained as the living core of the daily offices from Jesus' time to ours. Devout Jews offered prayers and psalms periodically throughout the day. Such services were a feature of synagogue worship in the days of the apostles. These Old Testament perceptions of time developed naturally into the church's "canonical hours" or "offices" at which time prayers were said in the form of psalms, hymns, antiphons, and responsories, along with the Eucharist. Together the Eucharist and Daily Prayers became known as "The Divine Office" (Officium Divinum), "Liturgical Office," or "The Liturgy of the Hours," as encased in "The Breviary," the Book of Hours.

DAY 2

Before Dawn (Vigils)

what was I made for

> how do I become again myself
> no longer crawling on the ocean floor
> how do I become that for which I was made
> before the flaming swords of Eden

> I dream of quiet laughter with you
> that was what I was made for

> I dream of dwelling in your presence
> filled with love and grace
> for that I was made

> nothing separates anyone from one
> who is inseparable from all

First Hour of Morning (Lauds)

beholding your glory

> beholding your glory in the tiniest creatures
> in amoeba seen only with magnifiers
> adoring your majesty in the silence of dust
> I feel your presence on the slip of a breeze
>
> what refreshment for the soul
> what relief amid daily burdens
> what joy amid dreadful struggles
>
> what incomparable pleasure
> above all earthly madness and passion
> you bring to your creatures
> simply by appearing at this feast

Mid-morning — Third Hour (Terce)

from egret heights

> looking out from the heights of snowy Egret Point
> the thunder shakes the deep fjords
> a one-eyed wanderer with broad-brimmed hat
> looks out upon the sea
>
> nothing needs to be added to the vista
> no missing piece
> except for her

Noon — Sixth Hour (Sext)

the long sea voyage

> I sit with a cup of hot tea
> lemoned and sweetened
> like this bright day
> sweet and stimulating
>
> I sit midday on the deck by the water
> living out a fantasy of a long sea voyage

surrounded by a splendid classic library
looking out upon the waves to calm and feed my soul

times when I have been most myself
are here with you out on the promontory
waves splashing

Mid-afternoon — Ninth Hour (None)

hollowed out

my head has become hollowed out by minutes ticking
empty of linkage
weary of remembering
pushing away from the desert shore of a vast continent
every muscle tired
grant a calm heart
over deep waters

Evensong (Vespers)

in evening shadows

why rage against the dying light
that comes as friendly servant

praise the One who gave the darkness
let it edify the soul
do not miss the tender glow of evening

the shadows wed clear blues with deeper greens
vanishing westward into thick darkness

the city is reflected in a ghostly halo of light
windows blush from the far side of the lake
that teems with life

Nighttime (Compline)

from my lips to your heart

from my dark valley to your unapproachable light
I scan the empty sky

from my weak eyes to your far horizon
I search for signals of your coming
from my wounded conscience to your lofty mercy seat
I plead for pardon
from my open arms to your bosom
I hasten for comfort
from my diverted glance to your all-seeing gaze
I cast an eye toward revelation
from my faint voice to your strong Spirit
I shout from a distant hill

I search all night
hoping for a bridge from my lips to your heart
to offer what I have and who I am
to who you most truly are

DAY 3

Before Dawn (Vigils)

when finally you return

> when finally you return
> you will reclaim all gone amiss
> restore your justice in the streets
> gather your wandering flock
> burn away all dross
> feast with your bride
> make right all wrongs
> just as you promised
> when finally you return

First Hour of Morning (Lauds)

where from here

> before the dawn
> nothing seemed possible
> entirely nothing seemed likely

I ask could you lead me from here

from nothing where is there to go
but return to you
you the incomparably present one
you the only one who does not flee
you who only can rightfully claim tomorrow
you who are exactly who you are
you who gently bound all my limits

take me from here into the coming day as you will
where nothing can become
but that which comes from you

Mid-morning—Third Hour (Terce)

let love stoop low

why do I still will to stand up high above
all that I love

why is it so hard to bend the knee
especially for me

this wayward will must be put right
this disordered love must be reversed
let your love stoop low

Noon—Sixth Hour (Sext)

the dexterity of the accuser

the detective is always only a few steps behind
the accuser poised in the back of the mind
conscience never rests
the apostle knew: it leaps ahead in mind's eye

the adversary knows exactly how to tempt with unrivaled
    agility
with skills honed from heaven to earth through countless
    ages
whose eye is able to see through mists from far away

whose cunning is beyond knowing
whose memory is bent but long

Mid-afternoon — Ninth Hour (None)

the concert of the willow leaves

astonished by the grandeur of the gentle willow limbs
moving gracefully against a placid sky
I am moved by your soft breath
through tips of willow leaves
in the almost silent breeze

the creatures of the marsh have joined me
in an evening symphony of sounds
the gull, the grackles, frogs, and geese close by
the sounds of commerce from afar

now quiet, now spirited the slender leaves move
with changing moods and colors
from deep green to bright gold they shine
remaking the light of the waning sun

Evensong (Vespers)

today now gone

an outlandish mockingbird melody
flung out into the wind
is spent on a dry moment unattended
an inimitable melody
never yet heard and never again

today my song has drifted with the wind
toward never or maybe

at last the sun is setting upon a yielded evening
today now gone
I once again am invited to be made one with you in time
you in whom nothing is lost

Nighttime (Compline)

shadowed freedom

> each step of my free decision is shadowed
> by all the competing conditions of human freedom
> with all the risks of finitude
> no moment spared
>
> the owl sees far into the night

———————————— **DAY 4** ————————————

Before Dawn (Vigils)

friends far away

> the friends I had long years ago
> I thought would be more with me now than then
> but now are ever farther away in both time and space
>
> restore me to my friends Lord
> bridge the gap of my pride and inattention
> change me
> that I may greet them again warmly
>
> it will someday be too late

First Hour of Morning (Lauds)

this very moment

> there will be winter days when I recall
> this dawn lingering upon the whitening blue
> as if a painter were constantly changing his pallet
> each moment newly inspired
> adding hints and traces of never before beheld hues
> never describable
> never imaginable until this very moment
>
> like the hidden day ahead

Mid-morning—Third Hour (Terce)

welcoming solitude

> the awesome gift of solitude
> allows me to be more fully present
> to you than all others
> to now than then
> to here than elsewhere

> this is no flight from human bonding
> to work and pray is not to flee the neighbor but serve
> toning the will to embrace the next one in need

> some may dread solitude
> but I thirst for it
> some feel its emptiness
> but I its fullness

Noon—Sixth Hour (Sext)

never

> under the cottonwood dying at its tops
> I whisper never
> yet the moment I say never
> I wonder if tomorrow I will say maybe

> the space between never and maybe
> is but a shadow of a hyphen

Mid-afternoon—Ninth Hour (None)

bracing for contingencies

> preparing for a distant voyage
> journeying alone to another continent
> speaking another language
> bracing for contingencies
> making hazardous decisions quickly
> arranging for absence from familiar duties

packing lightly for a long trip
scurrying to get ready
critics waiting three thousand miles away

I pray for a patient spirit
for a heart full of charity
anticipating long days ahead
in rigorous critical reflection

this lengthy journey seems like a detour
a burden and a diversion
a privilege now felt as annoyance

Evensong (Vespers)

where can I go from nowhere

where from here is an opening to the future
no path is yet laid bare
all seems impossible except for acts of imagination
nothing is set securely in history
except your continuing presence
with your unending grace in time

Nighttime (Compline)

a faint light glimmers

a faint light sparks randomly
throughout the night on restive waves
barely whispering to the coming day
seeking strength for perseverance
burying the soul with nothing more than promise

from these depths we rise
not yet but soon
to walk with new bodies
coming surely as the dawn
though long postponed in chilling winds

—————————————————— **DAY 5** ——————————————————

Before Dawn (Vigils)

you see all time as a single now

>
> to you who see all time as a single whole
> effortlessly
> I come with laboring heart
>
> the day has left broken memories
> its moments powdered into glimpses
> flashes of light blazing in the brain
> only to float away
>
> for you no moments are lost
> nothing unredeemable
> nothing forever gone
> since being God you relate to time
> in a completely different way than I
> being eternal you see time in a single glimpse
> all pasts and futures as if they were now
>
> your light has left the sky
> inviting sleep
> threading the loose ends of the night

First Hour of Morning (Lauds)

you who mark the sparrow's hunger

>
> you know the gaunt sparrow by my window
> in search of tiny grains buried in parched grass
> so you must know me also in my hungry search
>
> you dwell in light unapproachable
> transcending all in time and space
> overshadowing all our fleeting forms of knowing
>
> how can I approach
> you who mark the tiny sparrow's search
> able to count the hairs on caterpillar's legs

you enrich poor lives with your mere presence
you bless your lowliest creatures
with your majesty
by having become lowly in the flesh

Mid-morning — Third Hour (Terce)

tuneful gifts

> hard won through arduous hours
> taught through months of scales and harmony
> from theory to practice to polishing
> from how to move the fingers on the keys
> to grasping the structure of a diminished chord
> till I could play by ear
> hearing inwardly what my hands easily performed
>   outwardly

> I hear the deep chord of the morning
> grateful for the one who gave a mother's gift

> this simple gift has not left me
> never failed to be there at a moment's notice
> any melody once heard could be played instantly years later
> from harmonies imprinted in the brain
> without effort or reflection or preparation
> simply there in my mind with specific chords to match
> welded into muscle memory
> now it seems so simple

> yet strangers stand amazed
> as if some magic rain was showering upon me
> which I suppose it is
> delivered through the love of the single one who bore me
>   into time

> I have no brain of genius
> but have come to reason musically
> as if effortless and innate

what a rare gift she brought me through hours of practice
imparted by one who loved me without measure

Noon — Sixth Hour (Sext)

we belong to ordered time

the architect arrived with plans
for a quaint stone house built on a lake
close to trees, water, wind
where one gets closer
by being separated

this structure did not just happen
it was designed
to rest between two tranquil vistas on the water's edge
where wind entwines with many fragrances

from here distant bells can be heard
peeling from a far-off tower
telling us we belong to ordered time

Mid-afternoon — Ninth Hour (None)

real needs are small and few

you've left me nothing more to desire
but you in your glory
what more could I wish than what you've already given
to what brighter valley could I have wandered than to here
where could I breathe more deeply than this place
where real needs are small and few

Evensong (Vespers)

light flickers dimly across the moving stream

the brief moment of the evening's glow
gives not the slightest hint
as to its weight or harmlessness
its potential guilt or innocence
its lengthy augury

light flickers dimly across the moving stream
never to return
no hint as to its portent

Nighttime (Compline)

I breathe her name in silent fog

> it seemed I had almost forgotten her
> till I breathed her name into the silent fog
> without thinking
> I heard my heart pronouncing her name

> she returned to whisper in the night
> when all was still
> suddenly appearing
> through the thin membranes of broken memory
> as if always right there behind a veil

——— DAY 6 ———

Before Dawn (Vigils)

some do care

> some pretend to care
> but lasting for a moment
> drift out to sea

> but some do care
> those I name in my prayers
> those I know in my heart

> why do I feel they don't care when they do
> why don't I care more that they still care

> because the heart is twisted
> the will is bent

> create in me a clean heart
> out of love give me a new will

First Hour of Morning (Lauds)

help me speak the heart I know

> as I leave the ancient port for high seas
> help me speak from the heart I know
> of the love by which I am known
>
> there is no fit memorial for Cassiodorus
> who carried west your glory from the east
> but if there were he would demur
>
> the voice of Irenaeus is gone
> except in tattered copied manuscripts
> Eusebius and Augustine lie silent but for books
>
> yet some small fragment of my tongue is left
> to lisp the grandeur of your story in time

Mid-morning — Third Hour (Terce)

remembering old friends gratefully

> with dearest friends I offer my heart
> without compulsion to explain
> since I know they understand
> seeing my heart already
>
> by name I hold each of them up before you
> these dear souls scattered
> throughout the vast geography of a wilting memory
> extending even now an arm of comfort over untold
> > years
> they have prayed for me
> they know me well in all my shortcomings
> beholding them just as they are
>
> before you I offer an act of praise for your gifts to me
> through those who remain my vital links with space and
> > memory
> matchless to me for all time
>
> few know their quiet heroism as I do

few have heard their heartbeat as closely as I
no one knows who they are
except a few with whom I have been privileged to have
    entered
the sphere of their wide inner world

they have names
some gone, some still alive

I am defined by my friends
who know me deeper than the rest
given from your hand
you the incomparable friend who knows me best

Noon — Sixth Hour (Sext)

why am I not somewhere else

    my body is looking for some place
    where I can take all my senses as one
    to behold and feel what is just there now
    however small or frail
    know what is beautiful because it is most there

    the inner eye planted in me already
    longs to behold this exquisite moment
    that is why I am here now
    watching tiny patterns of wind on water refracting light

Mid-afternoon — Ninth Hour (None)

the bridge

    you are the bridge above the yawning chasm
    the light that suddenly appears
    when no step seems possible

Evensong (Vespers)

seventeen ways to look at sunsets

    as a door closing
    as time forgotten

as a leaf fallen
as an end of turmoil
as a beginning of rest
as a time for musing
as a relaxing muscle
as an eyelid closing to the sky
as a time to grieve
as a needful death required for the resurrection of the
     body
as an embrace of soothing grace
as a promise of tomorrow
as a court of judgment on the day's desires
as a receding symphony
as the end of a sentence lately spoken
as a finale to the storm
as a nodding head

Nighttime (Compline)

down to nothing

down to dust sinks all flesh
down to forgetfulness all history
every cell of every living body breaking into powder
falling to pieces
blown away
down to nothing
yet all destined to return to life on the last day

until that day
conscience sharpens freedom's waywardness

thank God I got closure
on the day

let me face now
as if my future were nothing
but you with me and a fresh dawn

———— DAY 7 ————

Before Dawn (Vigils)

how time will tell

> only the end will reveal the beginning
> what all time always tells will then appear

> only on the final day will this night's import
> come to clear focus
> be grasped rightly
> understood within the whole
> that recognition cannot happen till the end
> which mortals never know encased in time

> yet if the end is revealed already
> on the tree and in the empty tomb
> all things in time will be seen as already encompassed
> prized in the mind of the giver of time
> fulfilled already
> then time will be resolved in the mystery beyond itself

> then time will tell

First Hour of Morning (Lauds)

engagement and withdrawal

> when repose is buried deep in activity
> I seek solitude and silence

> over time I want to breathe a steady rhythm
> of activity and quietness
> engagement and withdrawal

> adrenal days are costly for the soul

Mid-morning — Third Hour (Terce)

cooked by time

> how pleasant to sit in the sun
> happy to be slowly visited by time

not wrestling with the deceiver
within myself or another

let the sacred word fill my body
funding energy for a single deed
that glows with clarity

Noon—Sixth Hour (Sext)

the shape of now

the sun takes time to melt deep ice
the waters are hugging low the rocky bed
the ripples are precisely turned
the rock walls round me were formed through untold millennia
the breeze comes and goes in random rhythms

from these elements the moments of life compound
in scenes variably combined of earth fire air and water
ever newly arranging each moment
in the precise shape of now

Mid-afternoon—Ninth Hour (None)

while trees invent the shadows

the trees are redesigning shadows
for the lakeside evening

tall pine greens define the jagged horizon
against a pale quiet sky

who will ever see
ever know
the rare look of this day
from this point in time

no one will ever again see
its matchless tones and contours
taste its distinctive flavor
no one will bathe in its unique glory
ever again be greeted by its stark contrasts and subtle shapes

Evensong (Vespers)

racing toward dark

> the great blue heron have sought their nests
> high in the trees
> the silence of the evening is descending on all things living
> racing toward dark
> the day glows
>
> the light does not yield quickly
> to the descending night
>
> what glory you reveal to weary eyes
> that you have allowed an unworthy witness to this moment
> which you remember eternally
> though all temporal eyes forget

Nighttime (Compline)

adversity as occasion

> every moment has its part in the whole
> every motive
> each consequence
> beheld and embraced by you eternally
>
> before you all things fall in place
> as if mountains kneeled
>
> I need not plead for your presence
> since you are always already here
> I pray only for a glimpse of your real presence
>
> you know already where you are going with me
> you know all possible outcomes
> you exist in an entirely different relation with future time
> than I
> so my perceived catastrophe today is your occasion
> to show again your provident care

PART 2

Book II:
Rediscovering Time

Thematic Focus: *Finding Time with God*

Learning the Gracious Life: *Saving Grace*

Cycle of the Second Fortnight
Third Week
Fourth Week

Third Week

Interlude: The Cycle of the Day

Vigils: The early hours of prayer before dawn.

Lauds: Praise at first daylight.

Terce: Mid-morning prayer at the third daylight hour.

Sext: Midday prayer at the sixth daylight hour at noon.

None: Mid-afternoon prayer at the ninth hour.

Vespers: Evening prayer at sunset.

Compline: The day ends with a prayer before bedtime.

The meditations of this book follow the daily pattern of the seven hours of classic Christian prayer:

Name of Office	Traditional Name (with Correlated Rites)	Usual Time
Office of Readings	Vigils (Nocturns, Matins)	Before Dawn
Morning Prayer	Lauds (Prime)	Dawn
Mid-morning Prayer	Terce	9:00 a.m.
Midday Prayer	Sext	12:00 noon
Mid-afternoon Prayer	None	3:00 p.m.
Evening Prayer	Vespers (Evensong)	Sunset
Night Prayer	Compline	Before Bedtime

These seven phases of daily time form the structure in which each personal meditation surfaces.

Vigils (Night) and Matins (Before Dawn)

The early hours before dawn are called *vigils*, when the visual world is dominated by darkness. The prayers of the faithful are enclosed in shadows and blessed by silence.

In early Christian times there were three watches or vigils of the night, each lasting about three hours. The purpose of the vigil is to protect the city or the family from attack and watch for signs of danger. Vigils, or periods of watching in the night, are prayers celebrated in the predawn hours awaiting the coming of the light.

The practice of praying at night has a long heritage. The psalmist wrote: "I rise in the middle of the night to glorify you" (Psalm 119:62; LXX 118:62). Christians continued this Jewish practice. It was reported of Paul and Silas that they praised God at night in prison (Acts 16:25). Jesus "spent the night praying to God" (Luke 6:12).

At this darkest phase of the cycle of time, the people of faith remember that human freedom has stumbled and fallen into sin, guilt, and death. The fall of humanity stains the whole of history.

The earliest Christians in the times of persecution held their assemblies in the night out of necessity, in order to avoid detection. The places where martyrs and saints died were often the very places where the people gathered to remember Christ's death. When persecutions receded and finally ceased, Christians were able to celebrate all their rites freely during the daytime. Yet the custom of night prayers which had begun out of necessity was retained from devotion and choice.

During the night those who expect the coming reign of God remain vigilant. When the Lord comes at a dark and unexpected hour, as promised, he will find the bride, the faithful, ready to receive him (Mt. 25:6; Mk. 13:35). The scriptural hope of the second coming of the Lord is rehearsed in the predawn time of vigils.

Morning Prayer (Lauds)

As the night recedes, the faint appearance of the sun approaches. This natural phenomenon gives rise to prolific spiritual insights and reflections. Dawn praise at first daylight is called *lauds*.

As night is in many cultures the symbol of emptiness and death, so it is remembered that Christ rose from the grave at the end of the night to reveal that the darkness of sin and death would end and a new life would begin. Lauds comes in the early morning when the sun is dispelling the night and the new day is born. Scripture portrays the morning sun as a symbol of Christ rising from the dead.

Lauds rehearses the resurrection of the Lord at daybreak. It is the prayer of the church as light returns to earth, celebrating the eternal light bestowed on the world by the Risen Christ. It is called *Lauds* because it rises to praise the gift of the day, the brightness of the early morning light.

All of creation is now seen from the fresh vantage point of resurrection. The hymns, psalms, and scriptural testimony received in Lauds reflect the new birth of the day, gratitude for new light. This hour breathes the spirit of radiance, glory, brightness, innocence, newness. "Let this hour," wrote Benedict in the fifth century, "which the Lord glorified by the splendor of His Resurrection, and in which the light of new grace and the sun of justice is given to the faithful, be always celebrated with divine praises" (Rule I, ch. 3). This is a time to thank God for the first light of creation which is now viewed in relation to the second light of redemption in Christ.

Saint Basil (†379) says in the Longer Rules (37, 3–4) that the morning office of Lauds is a reminder to us to dedicate the day's first ideas of the mind and the first emotions of the heart to God. We need not begin manual work or occupy ourselves with other cares until we have oriented all our thoughts toward God, saying with the psalmist: "It is you whom I invoke, O Lord. In the morning you hear me; in the morning I offer you my prayer, watching and waiting" (Psalm 5:2–3).

The first hour of light has been since the fifth century called *Prime*. The act of praising God in early morning continues to be very important during the first daylight hour after sunrise. It is viewed as the time of waking up, of rising energy, of spiritual preparation for the day's work and events. In Latin *Prime* means *first*; *Lauds* means *praise*. So Prime is a number and Lauds is an act (praise). Today the first hour is now more often called Lauds than Prime.

As Lauds begins the day with joy, Vespers ends the day with confession. If possible they are to be prayed in community and not omitted. Morning and Evening Prayer thus become the two crucial hours of the spiritual day. They share the decisive moment of the change of light — its coming and going. Lauds and Vespers are viewed as hinge hours of the day of prayer, the pivots on which the day turns.

Mid-morning Prayer (Terce)

Mid-morning prayer is at the third (Latin: *terce*) daylight hour. At mid-morning the faithful gather to pray, recounting the descent of the Holy Spirit at Pentecost (Acts 2:15). In this descent there was poured out such an abundance of grace that the apostles spoke in all languages, and everyone understood those who testified to the gospel in whatever language they spoke. As the tower of Babel had divided human speech, so the coming of the Spirit at Pentecost united all languages and cultures. Since the Holy Spirit knows all languages, the Christian mission began to learn to speak all languages. What the adversary had divided at Babel, the Spirit began to unite at Pentecost. Hence the core prayer of mid-morning Terse is this: Come, Holy Spirit. It is the third of the seven canonical hours, typically prayed about 9:00 a.m.

The faithful pray for strength as the power of daylight strengthens. The day of prayer and work begins amid increasing light. During the early working hours the believer prays for grace and serenity to maintain an attitude of humble service in the presence of God. The actions of work do not preempt prayer, but form the context for prayer. Those who live the life of constant prayer "should have specified periods for manual labor as well as for prayerful reading" (Rule of Benedict, 48).

This third hour is remembered in scripture as the time when Jesus was taken to Golgotha and nailed to a cross. "It was nine o'clock in the morning when they crucified him" (Mark 15:25). Readiness to participate in another's suffering is a crucial act of the Christian's working life.

The three short offices of the midday called "The Little Hours" fall between morning and evening prayer: (Terce, mid-morning; Sext at noon; None in mid-afternoon). *Terce* is Latin for *third*; *Sext* means *sixth* and *None* means *ninth* hour. Hence the pattern of Psalm 55:17 is performed daily: "Evening, morning and at noon I will cry and lament." In the Old Testament, as seen in Daniel 6:10, we find the key allusion to these three times of daily prayer: Daniel got "down on his knees three times a day to pray to his God and praise him." In the earliest church there is evidence that the apostles and early Christians prayed at these three times, either in private or in common, following Jewish temple custom. The Acts of the Apostles and the Didache of the late first century, as well as Clement of Alexandria, Hippolytus of Rome, and Tertullian of Carthage, all speak of these set-aside times of prayer. These were practiced in the monasteries of Egypt and Palestine, making them central to the order of time followed by the monks.

Midday Prayer (Sext)

The sixth (Sext) hour of daylight is noon. The sun is at its apex. Acts reports that it was "about noon" that Peter, following pious Jewish practice, "went up on the roof to pray" (Acts 10:9). By now the body needs food. This is a time of replenishment. This is when Peter had a vision of food. It is a time for earnest prayer to resist temptation, to keep from being overcome by the demands and pressures of mundane life. Alert attentiveness may be difficult. Basil commended Psalm 90 at this hour, with its reference to the "scourge that lays waste at noon" (v.6). In traditional monastic settings the noon meal is received in silence or while listening to readings from scripture or tradition for the purpose of "feeding the mind" while the body is being fed.

Mid-afternoon Prayer (None)

Mid-afternoon prayer is called *None* (rhymes with *bone*, Latin for *ninth*) and is celebrated at the ninth daylight hour (roughly mid-afternoon), a fitting time to pray for patience and staying power for the rest of the day. People of faith are called to pray and not grow weary. Weariness is countered by holding up life to the mirror of God's holiness. There is no hopelessness where there is periodic praise and confession in the presence of God.

At None, the natural daylight is beginning to decline. In mid-to-late afternoon, one is becoming visually aware of the gradual descent of the sun and light. It is fitting to begin to think more of eternity than time. The faithful recall the biblical theme of perseverance in grace looking toward the last things, the final making right of all of history's wrongs. It is a time to pray for resolve, for the strength to continue bearing fruit. Having passed through the mid part of the day, the need is to keep on going, faithfully to finish tasks.

As dawn is remembered for resurrection, mid-afternoon is particularly remembered in scripture as the hour of Christ's final sacrifice. "From the sixth hour until the ninth hour darkness came over all the land." About 3:00 p.m. Christ died on the cross and humanity was redeemed by his self-giving. It was at the ninth hour that Jesus quoted Psalm 22:1, "My God, my God, why have you forsaken me?" He then said, "Father, into your hands, I commit my spirit," and died. The curtain of the temple was torn in two from top to bottom. The earth shook. Tombs broke open, and the bodies of many holy people who had died were raised to life, and appeared to many people.

It was the disciples' practice to visit the Temple for afternoon prayers (Acts 3:1). This hour is particularly remembered as the hour of the day when Peter and John cured the lame man in front of the Temple. The faithful pray for the healing of all human infirmities at this hour of the day.

What remains awaits its time. It cannot be rushed: after None comes Vespers at sunset (Evening Prayer or Evensong), and then just before retiring, Compline, or the completion of the day of work and prayer.

Evening Prayers (Vespers)

Vespers, celebrated at day's end, takes on the glowing character of evening. The day is done. Work is finished. The mellow evening light is rich and beautiful. It is like the gold refined by the fires of the day, transfiguring our visual world and making it radiantly transparent for God.

This is the hour of refined wisdom, of resting in thanksgiving and confession after the struggles, triumphs, and failures of the whole day. The psalms, scripture readings, canticles, and hymns traditionally selected for vespers celebrate the maturing of life toward fruitfulness. The origins of this prayer time predate Christianity itself and are linked to the evening sacrifice of the Jewish Temple in Jerusalem at sunset. "Let my prayer arise before you like incense, the raising of my hands like an evening oblation" (Psalm 141:2).

As day draws to a close, the faithful give God thanks for all the good they may have done, admitting what they have failed to do, and confessing any failings of thought, word, or deed. *Vespers* literally means *shadows*. The time of Vespers is when lamps are being lit.

This is a Eucharistic hour because on this hour Christ instituted the sacrament of his Body and Blood. The Lord's Supper is the supreme, incomparable evening sacrifice. The faithful consecrate to God at the end of the day the full end of their lives and all their deeds. It is a time for recalling the gift of his body and blood given to fully atone for all sin of all who are truly penitent. Vespers is the sixth of the seven canonical hours of the divine office. Since originally fixed for the evening near sunset, it is also called Evensong.

Night Prayers (Compline)

The day ends with a prayer before bedtime. *Compline* comes from the Latin which means *to complete*. It is the last hour of prayer before retiring for the night. It marks the completion of our day and anticipates the fitting end of human history, and of our own lives. At the end of the day the believer lives as if at the end of time.

In that hour Jesus prayed in the garden of Gethsemane to be freed from deception. By doing so, he gave us an indication that we too are to pray to be freed from the deceits of the adversary. It is a time for saying with the Lord of glory: "Nevertheless not my will but your will be done." It comes at a late hour when we instinctively seek protection for the night.

This is the last opportunity of the day for the worshiping community, before retiring, to review the gifts of the day and receive the grace of God that envelops them. Compline consists of an act of repentance and praise, with appropriate psalms, hymns, and prayers for the night.

Compline leads back into the darkness of the night, but a darkness now filled with grace. It is not the alien darkness of sin that was remembered prior to the resurrection vigil at Lauds. It is not a darkness of anxiety focused on possibility, but a darkness of mystery enwrapping all time. It is not a darkness of judgment, but of rest. This is the darkness of God's mysterious presence, the abyss of his mercy into which he lets us fall to embrace us in sleep.

Compline is best viewed as a daily spiritual exercise of readiness to yield all to God's will. It symbolizes the readiness to yield all of life to God. As death is a kind of sleep, so is sleep a kind of death, but one that opens up the fullness of life and light. It is the fulfillment that pervades the canticle of old Simeon on the threshold of death: "Now Lord, you will let your servant go in peace, according to your word, for my eyes have seen your saving deed which you have set before all: a light for revelation to the Gentiles, and for the glory to your people Israel" (Luke 2:29–32). The faithful pray at Compline for "a peaceful night and a happy death" (Saint Basil, Longer Rule).

Those who wish to live fully to the glory of God will not neglect these periods of prayer both during the day and night. The fixed hours are a help to facilitate attention toward God at specific moments of time on behalf of all moments of time.

Three psalms are prayed each night at Compline: 4, 90, and 133. These are psalms to be prayed by heart, often in the dark. These three psalms speak of the meaning of the night, going to rest, dwelling in the shelter of the Most High, and the protection of God. They are well tested as fitting for the end of the day.

After Compline, when the father of the family blesses each one present, it is time to observe "the Great Silence," when all unnecessary conversation ceases. The hours of dark turn one's thoughts to rest in God. "I will lie down and sleep in peace, for you alone, O LORD, make me dwell in safety" (Psalm 4:8). To God is entrusted all the concerns and efforts of the day just passed.

The day's liturgy is the work of God (*opus dei*), taking us into the mystery of our Lord's death and resurrection and holding us there, sanctifying our lives and all we do.

———————————————— **DAY 1** ————————————————

Before Dawn (Vigils)

come soon

> come soon
> come tomorrow
> come early in the morning
> now if you will it
> yesterday seems already too late
>
> when you come stay
> purify entire
> make alive
> take captive darkness
> ignite the flame that burns the chaff
> recapitulate creation
> make again the world
>
> come without ceasing
> eternally there in your coming

First Hour of Morning (Lauds)

without flock or partner

> a bird in distant flight alone
> on a straight line by hidden design
> toward a place unknown
> flying high without flock or partner
>
> mirrored in that bird
> enable me to rise early in the morning
> fly directly, tirelessly, without annoyance
> toward the far distant meadow

Mid-morning — Third Hour (Terce)

hearing the word by ear like music

> moving spontaneously from analogy to analogy

comparing text to text
echoing from the heart of the beloved community then and
      now and to come
in harmony with the celestial choir
taught by apostles, saints, and martyrs
freely moving within the bounds
of ancient creeds and counsels
with the fathers who thrived in the love of learning
the classic teachers showed how to play
the songs of ancient scriptural melodies
reaching from the widest span of history
to the nearest point of breathing

in time the faithful learn to consecrate time
to think of God by ear like music
to economize chords by playing fewer notes
to reach the deeper subtlety of the timbre
that one may sing in clearer tone
the faith once received
with strict and true ear
for what is flat or sharp or out of tune

true hearing does not come
without practiced singing within the ancient chorus

the beauty of the chord is not heard unwillingly
without readiness to bend the heart to listening

Noon — Sixth Hour (Sext)

under sleeping leaves

    under the shadows of sleeping leaves
    I smell the dust of what was yesterday alive

    from such broken elements will rise
    the new man and woman on the last day

Mid-afternoon — Ninth Hour (None)

the wisdom of the wind

> let the winter day be green
> let the muse linger

> listen to the birds of the heart
> listen to the ripples of the river
> listen to the bitter wind
> listen to the day's end

> to hear the wisdom of the wind
> is to be in my right mind

Evensong (Vespers)

as leaves fall

> this year's leaf will not be seen again
> nor will any past moment
> but its root and branch will produce a thousand more
> in due time with poignant irony

> how foolish for a creature made for time
> to despair of freedom in time under finite constraints

> you give me this one earthly life
> wrought in a particular time and space
> as training for that life with you
> that promises to endure beyond all times

Nighttime (Compline)

the late evening guest

> the evening sky is filled with colored hints of glory
> inviting me to rest in her arms
> as if there only to please me
> without any merit of my own

> now the pink cloud turns into a bright copper hue
> moving at the pace of evening's gentleness
> so slow as to be almost imperceptible

if the evening were a young maiden I would seek her company
filled as she is with the sounds and glances of love
deep in her eyes from her heart

I have the whole evening as my company
a gorgeous guest enfolded with silk in soft tones
what more could I ask
how could I be more blessed than be in simple time unfolding

what is there to do now
but breathe attentiveness

DAY 2

Before Dawn (Vigils)

how do I know

within bound time I'll never glimpse
your free and full beholding of time
yet lacking no other ground on which to look
        ahead
I'm forced to trust that I am I and you are you
that you and I do not exist in fantasy but in truth

how do I know it is me
reaching into the night

what do I mean when I say "I"
what mystery lies shrouded in that spare name
how do I know it is not some false witness
        speaking
some counterfeit word plundering the gloom
but for the church catholic in its humble continuity
the "I" would be hardly recognizable
how could I know by myself alone
apart from the living word prayed for centuries
in freely bound community

what vast room for error in every calculation
what mystery clings to the widest truth known

First Hour of Morning (Lauds)

a cello singing

    fashion me as a cello singing with the hosts
    a cup from which truth might be savored at leisure
    a seal to be stamped into the walls of memory
    a flash of light before dawn
    holding fast to the silent pivot within the dance of
          time

Mid-morning — Third Hour (Terce)

a break in morning labor

    let the breeze go by
    watch it sculpt the surface of the water
    with more constant beauty than I can take in
    right here already
    in the moving colors of the stream

    the needs of the blessed faithful are small
    no clamoring
    no turbulent cravings to indulge
    nothing more to do than feel the breeze
    to hear the distant sound of children laughing
    to hear the flow of air move gently through the cottonwoods
    the water splash on granite rocks

    for me just food and sleep
    books and time to read them
    watching ideas spring to life
    makes for a simple life richly supplied

    there's nothing more urgent to be done
    than let the breeze go by

Noon — Sixth Hour (Sext)

the broken umbrella

    it now leans on dry stones

harbored from the wet wind's testing
out of service
asking only to be thrown away

it once had a splendid moment
offering cool retreat on hot sand
a welcome shield from wet weather
now it sits inert and useless

let me lean on these dry stones and learn

Mid-afternoon — Ninth Hour (None)

how fecund is deceit

> how fecund is deceit
> how ready to multiply through the night

> one fruit fly today
> a thousand tomorrow

Evensong (Vespers)

the next footing

> flying low above the breakers the great heron
> turns wing and air to glory
> the target is the next footing

Nighttime (Compline)

my heart moves like the wind

> dodging capitals and punctuation I write fragments
> because my heart moves like the wind

DAY 3

Before Dawn (Vigils)

the best gift

> born before dawn in a prairie village hard to find
> the best gift I've ever had is life itself

coming from God with coital grace

how could it be
that only a moment separates me
from all that is past

I still can picture the crib
in that very bedroom
where I was born
where I was offered time and means to grow

First Hour of Morning (Lauds)

introit

beside still waters
the soft late chorus soothes the soul
transports imagination
relaxing the bent spine
awakened by the strings of song
hearing fugues that Palestrina once sung at Maria Maggiori
I open my heart to you, Lord
to the rhythm of your glory
you say to me:
you will persevere through smoke and drought
blessed by long-planned providences
despite all waywardness
through cleansing fires without despair

come, Holy Spirit, transform the temperament inside out
make me new from within
confirm your pledge
stamp me as your own

Mid-morning—Third Hour (Terce)

carving the lake

the eye intently fixed
upon the matchless way
you chip and polish your creation

carving the morning lake
into brilliant flashing effervescences
ephemeral gems
sharing your glory through changing contours
drenched with light

Noon — Sixth Hour (Sext)

in trouble on a calm day

some creature is in trouble not far away
the voice shrieks the peril
whoever that is and whatever the trouble
I speak for the myriad creatures of the cove
asking help for one in trouble

Mid-afternoon — Ninth Hour (None)

suddenly leaves

leaves barely clinging to blackened twigs
now lately cover river and earth
suddenly tossed by wind
coloring the autumn day

give me grace to let go
to cast my future with the wind

Evensong (Vespers)

my eyes feast

my eyes feast upon the flowing pattern of the sky
savoring the shapes and slopes of the horizon
looking for life that lies hidden under cold dry winter
        leaves

let my voice resonate with the colors of the closing day
let all that is within me
be as calm and quiet as the surface of the lake

though it flows through sluggish veins
let this be my evening song

let words be dumb in the presence of your mystery

Nighttime (Compline)

home from Africa

> so much of a great hidden continent I missed
> so many faces I did not see
> eyes that I did not look into
> yet those I saw burned into my heart
> what seemed then a heroic struggle is now only a sigh

> now safely aboard I fold my hands
> in the quiet theatre of my conscience
> interceding for those I leave

—————————— **DAY 4** ——————————

Before Dawn (Vigils)

why death marks freedom's boundaries

> finite freedom without death is only a fantasy
> invented by despair

> deathless freedom would leave no room for any decision
>   of any import
> since any could be forever reviewed
> remade infinitely

> if any outcome could be infinitely delayed
> decisive time would lack meaning
> rendering life empty without finite choice

> so death marks freedom's boundaries
> without which one could play such clever games of delay
> as to make all choice meaningless

> finite freedom without death is only a fantasy
> invented by despair

First Hour of Morning (Lauds)

the book of hours

> dawn to dusk and into black night
> let praise rise as fragrance from incense
> through all the hours
> let the whole day be ordered to life with you
> the sanctification of time is what we are made for
> though flesh is always falling short

> so order my daily hours only once given
> no less than seven times
> as the psalmist was paced
> to live fitly in your presence

Mid-morning — Third Hour (Terce)

when I let my heart speak

> when I let my heart speak
> it whispers, shouts
> or groans from depths
> where the heart has its own reasons
> which reason does not know

Noon — Sixth Hour (Sext)

childhood haunts

> I return to old haunts where I drifted as a boy
> like the sycamore leaf lifted by the breeze

> the creek bed was my hideaway
> where crayfish sunned on wet rocks
> while I romped through the high trees

> I relish the memory of seasons there
> with family picnics in the hills
> a peanut butter sandwich in the arbor park
> while swarms of cousins took wing over wide-open spaces
> only a stone's throw from where I grew up

my life undisturbed by the specter
of any proposed future whatsoever

Mid-afternoon — Ninth Hour (None)

still at work

minding tiny ripples
slender turns of curving light
glanced upon by the sun
my mind is still at work
unraveling delusions
sitting still beside restless waters

Evensong (Vespers)

no human story is fully told

no human story is fully told
few even in a fragment
what bizarre egocentricity
for me to think my story should be told
as if another had some hidden duty to hear it
better to tell the truth about oneself when asked
or when it might benefit the hungry
not merely as expression of my inner yearnings
but simply for the sake of the truth

Nighttime (Compline)

let all my faults be shielded

I have nothing to claim as righteous
only rags
so bring my faults under the shield
of your blood shed for me

abide with me now and ever
you who are never threatened with corruption or diminution
your enacted word is truth coming now
to join me to redeem my infirmities

in this coming rest I entrust myself to you

─────────────── **DAY 5** ───────────────

Before Dawn (Vigils)

you who remember all that I forget

>   almost at the pace of being there
>   I am forgetting what has happened just now

>   just as your eternal presence now is always momentarily
>   appearing
>   so is it always seeming to disappear
>   to a past accessed only by memory and words

>   there is only a short time to coax memory into words
>   that slip away in time
>   disappearing most rapidly for those of us most quick to forget

>   thanks be to you for remembering all that I forget
>   bitter or sweet
>   embracing it all in your crucified and risen mercy

First Hour of Morning (Lauds)

breaking dawn

>   as I gaze up to breaking dawn
>   as stars are vanishing before my eyes
>   melting into the brightening sky
>   all is in readiness
>   nothing out of place
>   nothing more needed
>   but to meet the effervescent day
>   that brims with momentous choices

>   tonight there will be nothing more to do
>   only dream of what transpired
>   only tasting dear moments of recognition
>   only remembering you hour by hour
>   unveiling your creation

only living through your history
relishing time's easy flow
only resting through the night

for now the inviting day is full of possibility

Mid-morning—Third Hour (Terce)

the inferno blazes high

with spine wrenched as on a rack
the mouth force-fed with burning leaves
the inferno blazes high above the city towers
this medieval picture of the final day horrifies
it seems so out of date

but just then I met an addict
whose spine was wrenched
who was being force-fed
whose living fire blazed high above the towers

Noon—Sixth Hour (Sext)

changing shapes of sunlight

were I a tree I would be a willow beside still waters
were I a bird I would be a blue heron fishing near the
willow bank
were I a wisp of air I would play as a ghost upon the
surface of the lake
changing into shapes of sunlight in a single beholder's
eyes

Mid-afternoon—Ninth Hour (None)

the vanishing turtle

sitting beside still waters
pondering the dance of tiny waves illumined by the sun
a frozen floating object catches my eye
barely a tip showing
completely still

pretending not to be

it is the color of a king snake's head
the size of a submerged thumb knuckle
could be a living creature
or a mossy rock obscured
a waterlogged tree limb
maybe a snapping turtle
with crocodile eyes only peering above the water's
      surface

puzzled over the motionless point amid ripples frozen
      in time
I watch as nothing moves

I'll not know if it's a turtle
till the precise moment it disappears

suddenly it vanishes with a quick jerk to dark safety
so much alive you have to look quick to see it
nothing could be confirmed until the instant it
      disappeared
revealing its true appearance only by its disappearance

Evensong (Vespers)

registering attendance

    the bullfrog croaks his presence in this hidden valley
    declaring his attendance for evensong

    the skimmers ride the bank swells
    largemouth bass leap up for low flyers
    mosquito fish swarm beneath the surface
    carp recycle minute living organisms
    the woodpecker broadcasts his appearance

    so I register my presence in this tranquil valley
    what can I be but grateful
    that there is little more to do than signal my being there
    upon a meeting where all convened have equal voice

all present and accounted for

Nighttime (Compline)

as day wrestles with night

as day wrestles with night
I await your visit
your time to review with me the day's events
to render verdict on habitual tendencies
your judgment revealed and grace manifested
your holy presence in time
no one is listening
except the hermit thrush

—————————————— DAY 6 ——————————————

Before Dawn (Vigils)

the quick forgotten day

all that I have known
is draining into a deep canyon unseen
to be forgotten by all but you

all I'll ever know is quick forgotten
but for dim edges of awkward angles
muted under clouded mirrors

most of it I've forgotten too quickly to grasp
even the dawn is gone
today is sprinting fast

only glimpses remain

only to recede into the deep storehouse of memory
        forgotten
known only to you

First Hour of Morning (Lauds)

nothing before or since

> a day like nothing before or since
> this hour, this space, this color of dawn
> this smell of wind
> this sound of leaves
>
> never once before did you create this day
> nor ever again

Mid-morning — Third Hour (Terce)

find a quiet place

> today I seek out a quiet place
> to search deep within for the one who says "I"
> looking for you within myself
> myself within you
>
> having lived a busy life of mingling and blending
> it is not vain to cry out in a closet without human
>   hearers
> to whisper in your ear alone
> not for any other audience
>
> who is to judge this day but you alone
> whose holy presence I now seek
> let all other voices be silent

Noon — Sixth Hour (Sext)

redeeming time

> distracted from the tasks at hand
> I seem to be losing time forever
> spare time never to appear again
> each moment its own special treasure
> I do not want to pass one by through negligence
>
> what can I do to redeem time
> nothing at all ever

that is God's business

Mid-afternoon — Ninth Hour (None)

as light descends

as the heavy mood of midday lightens
as the blue tern wings back over the cove
as the breezes settle
as light descends
as shadows deepen I bear in mind
not once have you left me without witness
when I am teachable you have never failed as teacher
help me declare honestly what is plainly there before
     my eyes
your glory revealed in time

Evensong (Vespers)

the snow goose swims alone

the stallion runs freely on expansive prairie hills
strong and spirited but alone

from frigid distant waters
the snow goose swims alone midday
without a mate

the locust whirrs deserted in darkness
pleading for a rejoinder

so I without a mate
run free
swim the depths alone

Nighttime (Compline)

the way through darkness

as her hand by slow degrees draws out of touch
as her head turns silently away
as she is carried down the steps

as she seems to glance back
as her warmth takes distance
as she leaves entirely never to return

my world implodes
the song ends
only silence remains
breath shortened
heartbeat taut
my life is turned around
to who knows where
now up is down

help me walk again
learn to breathe again
find some new course you set for me
hear the beat of a rhythm that echoes through her absence
show me the way through this darkness

DAY 7

Before Dawn (Vigils)

you who entered time to redeem it

> it would not be you
> to offer me life
> but with no purpose

> you being you would not withhold meaning from time
> even if now hidden and long to be searched out

> it would not be you to let emptiness reign
> you who entered time to redeem the whole of it

First Hour of Morning (Lauds)

as leaves fall

> as leaves fall
> I feel a poignant irony

that this year's cherry leaf will not be seen again
nor will any past moment
but its root and branch will produce a thousand more

how foolish for a creature made for time
to regret its life in time

you give me only this one earthly life
wrought in a particular time and space
as training for that life with you
that will endure beyond all times

Mid-morning — Third Hour (Terce)

when never meets maybe

I whisper to myself
never
as if "never" could be a final word I have a right to say
as I sit beside the shedding cottonwood

the word never
echoes to the margins of my soul as if it
a mere word could close off something permanently

yet just as I whisper never
I know that tomorrow I will once again be saying maybe
and maybe even surely

clock time from never to maybe is just a blink
so swift it cannot be photographed or bought
much less described

O maker of all possibilities
turn around each daydream wrongly pursued
render null and void all that's gone awry

Noon — Sixth Hour (Sext)

a crushed rose

she has gone
disappeared

except in dreams
where she comes elusively
appears and disappears

she left no explanation
no note, no instruction
no hint of where she would be

so here I sit alone beside the tall shore grass
wondering where she went so suddenly
without a clue

yet later I would discover
she left a clue hidden in a sacred book
a crushed rose still perfuming
for me to discover years later
in a dry season

Mid-afternoon — Ninth Hour (None)

bending low

> there are tasks to be done
> but my heart is not there to do them
> reclining by the willow
> bending low to the water

Evensong (Vespers)

the thorn lodged

> this thorn lodged in my heart
> unwedge it quickly Lord
> loosen it from my throbbing flesh
> binding me up again with soft cloth
> that I may know how I became vulnerable
> open my heart to my wounded flesh
> that it may tutor me in patient love

Nighttime (Compline)

forever passing

> good night
> the race is finished
> night descends
> the curtain is drawn upon the day

> the world forever passing
> awaits your redemption drawing nigh

Interlude: Meditation as a Way of Speaking

Meditations, as the term is used here, flow out of a daily order of psalms and prayer. But they do not pretend to be that order. They are merely thoughts that come out of those psalms and prayers. They depend entirely on the scripture texts and intercessions and circumstances that awaken them.

They are not meant to substitute for liturgy. They do not pretend to be psalms. They are merely meditations expressed during the canonical hours, during those seven special times of day in which these moments call all to holy living, and mark them as sacred.

These are passing meditations where experience is squeezed to its core. They have been remembered like a breeze is remembered. They are passed on without elaboration. They have actually appeared in passing time, now gone.

Meditations arise out of life with God as set forth in scriptures. They are searching thoughts about a scripture text personally experienced. They are encircled by the prayers of the beloved community. There is no substitute for the Psalms that constitute the core of the cycle of hours.

The meditations here were written in different contexts, but their distinct location in time is what makes them what they are. They are experienced at times of day which are acknowledged by tradition as set-aside moments of recollection of divine revelation. They are but broken remnants of true moments scattered through the hours.

These meditations are personal expressions of my life in that cycle of hours. This is less a series of prayers made about the hours than exclamations made within them. They are candid personal meditations on my life in those moments. They do not say *read me without the psalms and liturgy*. Rather they attest how the prayers and psalms of the hours are being absorbed by me. This is who I am when praying the hours. They tell the story of one who is thinking and describing personal experience through the liberating framework of the hours.

Speaking of Freedom

When we speak of freedom — humanity's greatest gift — we do well to speak in the spirit of freedom — in a free way.

I prefer freely formed phrases where experience is packed tightly into words with the least possible visual obstruction, in the most economic form of conveyance, without rhyming, and without any pretense to be literature. The life of meditation does not always come in balanced meters or formal patterns or poetic phrases, a special gift I do not have, though I admire immensely those who do have it.

Why do I avoid normal sentence construction? Because these phrases are not normal sentences. They are not referring to ordinary mundane times and places but times and places that became illumined in relation to the source and end of all things.

They are distinguished from theology as such. They do emerge directly out of a whole life of theological teaching and reflection. But they are not to be understood as reasoned argument, only as testimony to experience. All I am trying to do is tell the truth I see in the time given me.

Hardly Poetry

These meditations are not intended to be critically assessed by aesthetic criteria as a poem or novel might be by a literary critic, but by the spiritual formation they may elicit.

If these meditations were accidentally put on a shelf of poetry, they would sigh for being out of place. They disavow the name of poetry, not because I do not appreciate the poets, but because I do not want to drag the honorable poetic genre down to some netherworld of crudeness.

The meditative mind has often been profoundly shaped by the poets. For me that means chiefly Shakespeare and Yeats, whose works I always read with awe. But when life with God is viewed as a literary experiment, it falls short of its own intent.

Taken independently each meditative act also lacks the full range of the elements of prayer, rightly conceived. That would mean a steady equilibrium of adoration, thanksgiving, confession, petition, and benediction. The beauty of that wholeness is not found here separately, but at best only intuitively and sporadically. They reveal only that slender part of prayer that is in the Bible called *haga* or *siyach*, to ponder, murmur, reflect, meditate. They provide only glimpses of a more fully ordered traditional expression of prayer. That pattern can be found classically in the Psalms and scripture and the ancient liturgies, and the classic litany of the hours. These are cast in the form of free-flowing meditations touching upon life with God.

More Like Runes

They are more like puzzles than reasons. In Nordic tradition they might be called runes, sometimes translated puzzles — enigmas. They ask only to be pondered, not solved.

There is no lofty motive or systematic rationale for these runes. They are without scholarly merit. They are lacking in all of the features of compelling argument, in all the elements of good rhetoric, in any effort at persuasion.

No one could mistake a report card for poetry or a scream for therapy or a glimpse of color for a great novel. What arises from the heart is neither argument nor story nor healing. So what is it? Being honest to God.

Do not imagine I am here talking with myself alone. This is a conversation with real partners in earnest dialogue. One partner is infinitely more real than myself, the other less real than I would want her to be.

These recognitions came in brief moments like a dream half remembered, vanished before being examined.

Here there is no beginning or conclusion, few complete sentences, only phrases boiling up from the fire inside, as incense penetrating an undefined space. Here there are few pretenses of organization or plot or purpose or development or demonstration. Only musings that have awaited long nights for the muse to awaken. Only hopes that ply the water's surface, only dreams that cling to the far edges of consciousness.

Those seeking practical advice are cautioned: there is nothing to embrace but smoke that curls and drifts on the breeze. Just watch the smoke curl. There is little here except a thin film of refracted reality. If you step into the stream, be prepared to drift and flow and maybe at length sing and glory in what is.

Thirsty for the Spirit

Like Kierkegaard, I yearn not so much for a multitude of readers, but only that single one exceedingly thirsty and already stumbling in a desert. I have been in that desert. I know a hidden place to dig for cold clear water. I look for that one single companion as thirsty for the Spirit as I.

It does not ultimately matter a lot whether someone or no one is listening. It often seems better for my soul if no one noticed than if what is noticed becomes misunderstood.

Offered in these lines: petals drifting on the waves.

I have little to give another that I cannot better offer to myself. I am old enough to say what I think and feel without fear, but do not wish to compel anyone to ask my questions.

Those who pass by are at once invited and warned: come and go at your own risk, without knowing where the path will lead. Be aware. You are always leaving traces of your own footsteps. What you will find here are merely soulprints.

Fourth Week

——————————— DAY 1 ———————————

Before Dawn (Vigils)

hardly alone

> you for whom I sing
> at last the night is quiet enough to hear
>
> the tree that falls alone still falls
> nothing is ever unnoticed entirely
>
> God sees to that

First Hour of Morning (Lauds)

how well you know my ways

> how surely you know my destiny
> how brightly your light shines upon my footsteps
> how gently you hold me close to the path
> how softly you enter into my presence
> how carefully you soak and scrub and rinse
> to cleanse my corruption with your mercy
> how wisely you correct my errors
> how firmly you embrace my uncertainties
> how well you know my ways

Mid-morning — Third Hour (Terce)

hearing previously unheard chords

> thinking God
> arises from the heart
>
> the richest chords echo
> from two thousand years of sacred text
> no need for paper notes or promptings

they come instantly from the soul attuned
to the most ancient witnesses

the faithful think God
within the gathered chorus
hearing previously unheard chords
received and transmitted within the eucharistic
       circle
as an arpeggio played spontaneously without a score
coming from the deep soul alive
within the beloved community
comparing text with sacred text the chords modulate
ever new ever most ancient

prayer's most sure mentors died long ago
or so it seems
Basil, Gregory, Climacus
their graves unmarked
their instruments decayed
but their music still is heard
the fugue plays on endlessly

Noon—Sixth Hour (Sext)

under heavy winds

    what kept me upright under heavy winds
    but the single step I saw immediately before me
    that small space closely illumined by your word
    without knowing where I was being further led
    your lamp illumined that one step continually

    what held me close when I was wandering far
    but a thin and tangled thread through a dark maze
    that drew me
    your providence preserved that thread

    what brought me to today through hazardous time
    but you the giver of time
    without my knowing

Mid-afternoon — Ninth Hour (None)

awakening Lazarus

> in a venue almost forgotten
> the faithful plod on into the day
> remembering the phrases of the psalms
> clinging to unnoticed threads of resilient truth
> threads based on disappearing evidence
> yet growing daily in plausibility

> they beg for timely speech
> they shout to Lazarus
> already four days in the grave

Evensong (Vespers)

nothing to speak of

> what is going on
> nothing unusual
> only time touching eternity now

> really nothing to speak of
> unless the baptized soul is awake

> when you are already there
> in time touching eternity
> everything is always new

> so now breathe the evening air
> lungs filled with energy ready to receive
> willing to live
> glad to have time
> not pretend to make time

Nighttime (Compline)

embrace the night

> as sky melts into evening
> the silence descends upon the cedars
> the retreating sun leaves no regrets

enable me to release my grip
let go the day
embrace the shadows
yield without remorse
to the last blush of radiance
awaiting tonight's turning moon

———————————— **DAY 2** ————————————

Before Dawn (Vigils)

still growing

 like fingernails in the crypt
 we continue to grow
 even in the grave
 revealing the hidden vitality of tiny cells
 thought to be dead
 but unready to die

First Hour of Morning (Lauds)

the failure of metaphor

 the metaphor of seeing does not describe
 your grasp of all time
 but points to the wholly different way
 you see all time simultaneously

 the metaphor of mercy does not describe your mercy
 but points only to what we can know
 of your infinite kindness revealed

 the metaphor of knowing does not describe your knowing
 but points to what little we can grasp of your knowing

 the metaphor of justice does not describe your way of judging
 but points to the incomparable holy love you demonstrate on
   nailed wood

 the metaphor of power falls short of your insurmountable
   ability

to speak of your power is to point beyond power
toward that unique sovereign freedom
that precedes and transcends all creaturely powers

come now with your mercy and wisdom
power, foresight, and justice
come risen Lord

Mid-morning—Third Hour (Terce)

silent as the great white heron

a stunning slender white figure on the green bank far away
the great white egret stands motionless
not as a frozen marble statue lacking ability to move
but like a great living creature that moves
just when and where it wills

let my soul be still like this great white shore bird
untroubled by moving waves or changing skies
ready to meet all variations with gentle dignity

my muscles are not under such command
but quiver, jerk, and move unevenly
unlike the nobility of the great bird
pausing silent on the far shore

Noon—Sixth Hour (Sext)

finding voice

distracted I went far off track
in a dry season wandering on the sands

how did this happen
to one who sought your comfort

you had a hand in it
not without purpose
you introduced me to myself again
through that long journey
you were there to guide

with fire and cloud and manna
every step however bleak

at last I have found my voice
after forty nights of silent waiting
lingering mute like Zechariah in the temple

I now remember how it is to have speech
to become again like Adam
naming the objects in my world

Mid-afternoon — Ninth Hour (None)

the pilgrim returns

the pilgrim returns
full of wonder
tired and pensive
to smell dusty grass
listen to time
to breath and once again belong
not be misplaced abroad
but to be bathed in reflections of light from the shore

to enjoy the swimming parade of shore birds
two by two with all their young
in the evening faithful as in the morning
each fulfilled by the other

Evensong (Vespers)

two lives have intertwined

what have you put in us, Lord
that we so adore those we love

the irony is that this is home
the end for which our two lives have so long intertwined
yet only one remains

lacking a partner with whom to share it
I still enjoy it with and for her

as if she were here now
her absence seems incidental
her presence more real than her absence

what enchantment have you put in us, Lord
that we so adore those we love
through whom we are fulfilled in fondness
sustained through time beyond death

it remains a mystery
which I hold up before you
toasting its incongruity

Nighttime (Compline)

then sings the mockingbird

late falls the shadow on the wing
so stands the weight of time above the sun

then sings the mockingbird
lending music to the skies
late and soon the nights go by

so comes the ancient story to a last full stop
so marks the choir a gentle benediction
so falls the impress of your final stamp on time

─────────────── **DAY 3** ───────────────

Before Dawn (Vigils)

the wind rises

I saw the wind pushing the water back upstream
tossing earth to sky
trees wrestling with air
I saw thin air bending heavy branches
shaking mighty trees to their deep roots
I saw the swift movement of time
flowing toward the eternal now
the wind blows where it pleases

not as if nature chooses intentionally
a powerful natural force not to be hindered
everywhere relentless
wherever it chooses to move
no one can grasp the wind
even with strong fingers

when the wind rises we know it
but from where we know nothing
the Spirit cannot be held or encompassed

though aware of his presence when he comes
the reasons for his coming and going remain a mystery
leaving only the ghost of his company in our ears

First Hour of Morning (Lauds)

remake me

refashion now the sinews of my heart
fit me for tomorrow
renew my soul
resurrect my bones to active life

how in coming to be
do I come to be better
while in coming to be better come not to fall
while in falling return again not to stumble

remake me

Mid-morning — Third Hour (Terce)

nothing is required

nothing is required
but daily life in you
breath by breath
in simple obedience to your living Word
full attentiveness to your distinct new call each hour

unfettered sacrifice of everything now
birthing the freedom to praise

Noon—Sixth Hour (Sext)

she left me herself

> when misplaced hopes come to nothing
> descend into a dark abyss
> flee forever with no calling card
> no forwarding address
> just absence
> aching empty absence

> that is how it seemed when she left
> when she was taken away

> later I realized how mistaken

> she left me herself
> her memories
> her love
> her children
> her very self for me alone
> her endless gifts of spirit

> the woman is the glory of the man
> so scripture says

> she was and is my glory

Mid-afternoon—Ninth Hour (None)

let me settle my accounts with you

> you who have invited me and I have come
> command the heights of my defenses

> help me settle my accounts with you

> I have no place to stand on which to call you to account
> because you are sovereign Lord
> maker of conscience

> how late in the day
> to settle my accounts with you

if I ask for justice you might give what I deserve
so I plead for mercy

God help me
you who have taken all my debts upon yourself

Evensong (Vespers)

the eagle soars the mountain valleys free

    once the eaglet lacked strong wings to fly
    squawked to be fed
    at risk cliff side
    imagination going wild

    through countless living animal sacrifices he grew
    to let wings spread against the wind
    to test the strength of air
    to lift him to snow heights

    now the heart of the eagle soars
    seeing miles across the valley
    diving instantly a thousand feet for prey
    bursting with strength and quickness
    opening up the heavens
    diving to the depths

Nighttime (Compline)

reshape my wayward freedom

    the free grace offered in the night
    is more than I deserve
    coming quietly to my heart
    as a calm instructor in the still dark hour
    counseling patience in love
    perseverance in hope
    lit by fires of faith

    so coach me in tomorrow's larger plan
    guide me for useful employment

train me for heavy lifting
discipline me for the race

move me unmoved mover
mold me unseen architect of the will
reshape my wayward freedom
for living under grace

spinning through the obstacles under my feet
enduring to the end

DAY 4

Before Dawn (Vigils)

night

the voices of the natural order are still
excepting frog and cricket
proclaiming your glory even in blessed silence

now let your servant go in peace
in a night without a star
a cloudy, deep, dark night

while trees still breathe your sovereign love
while waters silently refract your light
while the echoes of the evening trace your word in time

First Hour of Morning (Lauds)

no door ajar

I cannot see an opening to the future
no door ajar
no path already made
all things seem impossible
except for my imagination

nothing set in time seems secure
but your continuing presence
your patience mending grace in time

Mid-morning—Third Hour (Terce)

where I come from

I once found a squalid home
in the streets close by the Bastille
strumming the five-string banjo with Woody Guthrie
of goons and ginks and company finks
and deputy sheriffs on parade

once bitten by utopian dreams
with a belly ache of Nietzsche
mesmerized by the rhetoric of conquest
grazed blithely on Rousseau
thirsting for supposed revolution
pretending to welcome heroic violence
imagining myself at home with the conspirators

this is where I come from
God help me for the poisonous dreams I introduced
to others

Noon—Sixth Hour (Sext)

brick by brick

why is it so hard
to build brick by brick
with muscles sapped and sinews worn
why so hard
to hold true course
against the hostile gales
despairing over freedom's costs
so cries the voice of rage

why so hard to persevere
on the way toward the far mountain
with so many distractions in sweetly cushioned
meadows
so cries the voice of bitterness
complaining of freedom's limits

pleading for less range of choice and consequence
than risk-laden finite freedom requires

enable me Lord to build brick by brick
walk step by step

Mid-afternoon — Ninth Hour (None)

she was like that

how pleasant she has made my lonely moments
how cleverly she has done what she has done
bringing laughter, tears, insight, amusement
put an end to boredom
if for an hour
sung, mimed, and danced her way into my heart
so I will never forget her
and will be forever grateful

how did she know just how
to touch my heart
to jerk my soul from my shoelaces
to drain my emotions
to awaken my compassion

she was like that
my only love as full of comedy as tragedy
of song as weeping
she brought to me the full range of sensation
made transparent through her face
her eyes
her voice
the language of her body
the laughter of her soul

Evensong (Vespers)

loose words

I wrench the words from my heart
since they do not form easily on my lips

I pry them loose from heavy moorings
buried deep in layered defenses

loose words
I now look at them as if holding a snake in my hand
when the smell of mendacity has lingered on my fingertips
you know every one every time
every evasion

teach me to be attentive to my loose words
help me state the simple truth

through conscience you bring shame to my shamelessness

Nighttime (Compline)

a widening flood of silent words

> this night gives little solace to the soul
> the morn seems overdue

> a wall of weighty books stands silent through the
> > night
> while heavy flooding chokes the seeds of sleep
> where words pour forth without recognition
> spilling like a broken river dam

> let me be patient in the night that light may come
> illumining the actual contours of a new day
> that will reveal the status of the times
> still shaking over the widening flood of silent words

> the birds will fly tomorrow
> whatever I imagine tonight

—————————————— DAY 5 ——————————————

Before Dawn (Vigils)

now comes the dawn

> now comes the dawn
> inching slowly into the welcoming day

soaking up lost time
placing its new claim upon the yielded earth

let me not miss your coming
let me not be sleeping when you appear
let me not be deadened by history's corruptions when you
      are revealed
let me not spend my budget of short time thoughtlessly
let me not come into your presence with anything withheld
let me not pretend to be able to evade your righteous
      judgment
let me not foolishly seek to hide from your view anything
let me not be dull of mind at your unannounced
      appearance
let me not welcome you shabbily
let me sing heartily with all the angelic voices on your arrival
let my life be ordered at your coming
let my actions not bring shame to your glory
let me not come into your presence without the proper
wedding garment

First Hour of Morning (Lauds)

the topmost leaves are curling

    the topmost leaves are curling
    in the sun high above the trees
    reddening, cooking
    parching in the wind

    they know that winter comes quickly
    that they must brace and be outfitted spare
    with all the hope that spring has given
    with all the strength that summer yields
    with all of the moist roots early autumn has provided

    open my eyes now to what is happening
    to acorns, trees, shrubs
    late flowering plants and grass

behold the vivid panorama soon to disappear

Mid-morning—Third Hour (Terce)

where could this possibly lead

no exit or conclusion seems evident
the trend of time seems imponderable
the end submerged in primordial ash
the goat still ravenous
the finish undefined

yet the offer of compassion remains
even when the shape of tomorrow is unforeseen
when the time of futility boils the fat to nothing
when nothing appears possible

meanwhile you laugh from heaven at our folly
knowing the certain end of all deceit

Noon—Sixth Hour (Sext)

the normal wounds of finitude

suddenly the sting of the wasp
shoots toxic fluid in my veins
leaving a whelp that remains unabsorbed
setting off itching soreness

the wasp has no regrets at all
just according to his nature

it comes and goes quickly
but its mark remains in me a while
festering and sore

help me bear the normal wounds of finitude

Mid-afternoon—Ninth Hour (None)

you lifted me

you are the source of my courage
the ground of all my striving

the hidden root of my hoped harvest
you accompany me in the journey
you lift me over dangerous rocks
you save me amid perilous waters

let the earth sing your praise

Evensong (Vespers)

the cost of damages

the cost of damages from careless speech
is three to one on forgiving days
only six million brain cells have been set afire
by what I've hastily said

I have more to spare
yet thank God not inexhaustibly

Nighttime (Compline)

it is time for silence to rule

it is time for silence to rule
for creatures to seek safe places from human promises
for bone and flesh to sleep
for dreams to enter and flow and fill the night

so let my heart be silent
let me find a safe haven
let striving cease
let silence rule
let dreams enter and flow and fill the night

—————————— DAY 6 ——————————

Before Dawn (Vigils)

be present with us in the flesh

gather us into your huddled flock
bring us through the gate into the fold
come again to draw us toward you in love

keep us by night for the coming day
come again to vindicate your purpose in unhurried time
come again to be present with us in the flesh
to rule the powers of darkness
to receive your own children into the kingdom of light
to end suffering, death, and guilt
to bring all the broken hours to full and fitting fruit
in the light of who you are as merciful judge

you mend our failings

First Hour of Morning (Lauds)

overflowing

    like an overflowing cup I spill over
    with gladness for all that is
    without reserve affirming finite life
    lived within firm and cordial boundaries

Mid-morning — Third Hour (Terce)

the dangerously fruitful brain

    like semen by the billions
    the brain floods with untested ideas
    each pretending to promise something better
    with all but the minutest portion falling short
    creation's fecundity allows this abundance
    to provide the species durability in time

    cursed and blessed by our generative powers
    we spend our fleeting energies and passions
    hoping you will bring forth fruit from our flesh
    aware that the gift of freedom bears danger

    seeing that freedom since Eden is prone to fall

Noon — Sixth Hour (Sext)

no need to rage

    I shade the eyes from the high sun

enough to glimpse time meeting eternity
I turn away from the sun
feel the cool grass beneath curled toes
hear songbirds in tree tops
feel gentle breezes through the leaves

there is no need to rage at time's relentless flow
or stem the tears that sometimes rise within

Mid-afternoon — Ninth Hour (None)

the muses

imagination loves possibility more than life
but if lacking possibility
even some fantasy of something possible will do

the muses breathe in forest dreams
fleeing when throats are dry
they do not sing for nothing

the Dionysian muses thirst for untasted moments
always on the edge of the new
they cannot abide the boring
there is no marching in the forest
no storage bins
only now

Evensong (Vespers)

grateful to you for her

a word spoken low
a look that went straight through me
a glance that stormed my heart
a sigh that echoes in my memory

it was her depth of soul that she so freely revealed
that I alone was privileged to know as dear
to live with
hold close

so elegant
allure does not begin to say it

Nighttime (Compline)

I taste tomorrow in the night air

already as if here
sweet to the tongue
with low sounds falling softly
scented to the palate
delicate to the lips
I taste tomorrow in the night air

———————————— DAY 7 ————————————

Before Dawn (Vigils)

what if

with waning energy
I wonder what earthly weight I now must bear
without yielding to despair

when I stand near the abyss of deadly possibility
the cost of anxiety is dear
detracting me from the assigned path
though tempted I do not despair
hardly for a blink
since you encompass my life with hope

First Hour of Morning (Lauds)

the way of the wind

when mirth jests with darkness
when dancing slips through waves
when music tunes the cosmos

then laugh with time
let singing lift the heart
let dancing follow the way of the wind

Mid-morning—Third Hour (Terce)

the trial of trees

in the trial of the tallest trees
each struggles to hold to its roots
against the complaint of blustery winds

the loftiest limbs are stripped bare
by a force so airy light it cannot be seen

it has been a dazzling day of bright light
swift movement
harsh display of force and fury

each tree knows its strengths are deep
its frailties high

Noon—Sixth Hour (Sext)

struggling to breathe

any glimpse may be the last
I wipe the sweat off my face
tongue dry
face buried in hands

what was once fully alive is struggling to breathe
I must somehow trust my common sense
despite all rational arguments
as the tiny creature struggles up the rainy slope
looking for purchase

Mid-afternoon—Ninth Hour (None)

ecstasis

I hear myself uttering a sentence
with no period at the end
no verb in the heart
no sentence structure

only ecstasis
in a tranquil cove

at a delicious moment
in a calm mood
after a hazardous day
with the wind at rest

Evensong (Vespers)

Sabbath rest

there is no need to take time
but only to let time take me
rocking me into stillness

let this time put its stamp upon me for eternity
bear me through the wind

nothing has come to pass
unable to be blessed by God
brought by steps into a redemptive purpose

the whole person refracts the whole day's light
like the river at the end of the day
flowing toward the final day of rest

Nighttime (Compline)

at day's end

come Holy Spirit
refresh the labors of this day
bless useful gleanings
bring me ever nearer to your call
to sketch anew the faces of the saints and martyrs
for those who live today
bring me within range of beholding you
that I may celebrate in you already
the fitting consummation of all that is

now let your servant depart in peace
that peace may be received in lives of strangers

Interlude: Private Prayer Grows Stronger within Community

Whether physically within a community of prayer or in a solitary closet praying in the spirit of the community, I am with the community. Praying through the hours always occurs within this community. Even when alone, I pray with these dear companions stretched over generations.

When we speak of this community of faith we point to a community of prayer sustained over millennia of expectation and fulfillment, the great cloud of witnesses from Abel to Abraham to Paul to Clement to magnificent holy women with soft names like Macrina and Teresa. It is the community of the prophets, apostles, saints, and martyrs. It includes believers in the historic Jewish and Christian community of witnesses to God's coming in history.

When I raise my heart in solitary prayer I raise it within and with this actual community. Singing with them does not require their physical voices, but the spirit of their life of prayer, located always within the spirit and inspiration of that ongoing community through millennia of time.

The Hours for Busy People

Lay Christians in their busy daily vocations in the workplace as employers, employees, laborers, managers, and moms may not be free to observe the liturgy of the hours strictly in the traditional way or utter these prayers or walk in this way visibly or in a common worshiping community.

Those pressed by overwhelming demands of their vocation may complain that this approach to time is difficult to carry out, too expensive, demanding too much effort. But what is truly valued without effort? If slavish, then prayer is not rightly ordered time. It need not be followed mindlessly. The practice of these hours may become an oasis of rest for any who are wandering.

The people of God are found doing battle against the spiritual powers of darkness at any time of day or night in a way fitting to that shade of light or darkness.

These are meditations for laity on the classic Christian hours of daily prayer. They serve as an internal clock to call the believer to prayer throughout all the day, letting all of life be suffused with the glory of God. They offer a contemporary way to practice the ancient biblical tradition of hallowing time throughout the day. These meditations show how through a busy life the hours of classic Christian devotion may be folded into the varied times of a turbulent day.

The Longing to Flow with Time

These hours have surged and coursed and drained through every vessel of my spiritual growth. I do not dare say that any other should follow them. I only know that I have been bathed in them, like waves returning to the shore.

To those not strongly motivated, the scriptures make this modest promise: You may if you wish draw closer to solitude by praying for divine grace to be responsive to whatever gifts are here and now offered.

Stay within this tested pattern of prayer. Try it for a day before committing for a week. Try it for a week before committing to a series of weeks. Test it for a season before committing yourself fully. Those who feel they are not ready for any commitment whatever can still pray for the grace to become ready for it.

Some may view themselves as liberal or evangelical or catholic or something else — it doesn't matter. Some may be prone to turn the gift of prayer into either a routine duty or a passing feeling. Praying through the hours promises to help overcome both the legalism and sentimentalism that may dilute life with God.

These meditations seek to set out a simple map for the journey. They are for those who have never been introduced to the classic ecumenical pattern of timely Christian prayer.

Praying through the hours is not a command but a gift. Those who enter this house as a duty will find that they become slaves in this house, while those who enter this house as a sheer undeserved gift will find that they become sons and daughters of this house, and heirs of its treasures.

PART 3

BOOK III:
THE CLASSIC CHRISTIAN
HOURS OF PRAYER

Thematic Focus: *Being Found by God in Time*

Learning the Gracious Life: *Consummate Grace*

**Cycle of the Third Fortnight
with a Completing Seventh Week**
Fifth Week
Sixth Week
Seventh Week

Fifth Week

—— DAY 1 ——

Before Dawn (Vigils)

whence all this light

> whence comes all this light
> isn't it deep night
> yet even now glints of light are breaking through from
> > somewhere
> it seems from nowhere

> could it be from some obscure source far across the lake
> beyond the lake
> beyond the earth's horizon
> beyond this galaxy
> beyond all beyonds

> maybe
> but not from nowhere

> from you, Lord, flows all light
> even the tiniest flickers through the night

> all lights in time and space
> show forth mirrored refractions of your incomparable light
> made known in a fleshly history
> coming as light of the world
> by which all other colors, shades, and textures are lit

First Hour of Morning (Lauds)

without pretense of virtue

> when I come into your presence pretending virtue
> yet stained by pride
> so easily recognized by those who know me best

whether glimpsed at the edges or smelled rotting from
     the core
then I know

you know me all the more wholly
than best friends and critics

it is no simple art to hide worst vices
but with you no cleverness avails
into your presence I cannot come
without you knowing all

so now I come before you wholly vulnerable
asking pardon for all I've done and not done
for all that echoes through future time
in discord with your will

Mid-morning—Third Hour (Terce)

the hours are full

> with you
> incomparable one
> the hours are full
> brimming with mercy, kindness, help

> you alone are worthy of worship
> with you the daylight hours are full
> with me the hours are made full by your fullness

Noon—Sixth Hour (Sext)

speech embodied

> wake up my speech
> to say what simply is

> let it be embodied in my steps

Mid-afternoon—Ninth Hour (None)

least likely

> isn't the judge who himself is willing to die for the accused

the one least likely to condemn the accused for whom he
    himself died
to whom he has promised that his word could be trusted

if in my dying breath
someone offered his life for mine
that would bind my conscience

if I ask another to trust my word
would I then let that very one who trusted me stumble
so it is with you who gave your life for me

in this way we are most contented
to return your offering to us
by relying wholly upon your self-offering

Evensong (Vespers)

feasting upon memory

the summer visit of the snowy egret
that dwells on the far edge of the lagoon
ready for edibles as they appear
now walks on stilts by the secluded lakeside
calmly stately undisturbed

you bless me with the sounds of serenity
the quietness of evening
the smell of growing grass
the freshness of the passing day

let all this enter into my body
to be feasted upon by memory
that I may reflect the glory of this evening

Nighttime (Compline)

plead my case

when all options seem closed except to keep on walking
when nothing lies ahead but a darkening haze
when time is spent yet timely accounts cannot be delayed

accompany me through the testing
as my advocate
clothe me in your mercy
walk with me through the fiery ordeal
pleading my case as if your own

DAY 2

Before Dawn (Vigils)

you permit my folly

you do not intrude upon my freedom to be foolish
you give me time and space and let my freedom play
skewed and off center
knowing you will right the better outcome

but for now you let the game of choice play itself out
freely

you accompany me in the valley of foolishness
you do not withhold your grace amid my folly

by this you prove your sovereignty
by this wildness your wisdom is glorified
by this disorder your higher order is attested
by this you conquer my soul
by this you claim all of me without reserve

First Hour of Morning (Lauds)

surely this world could not be the best

is it better to live with freedom's curse
or without freedom's blessings

surely it seems
this world could hardly be the best you could do Lord

could this day be the best all things considered
is it better than a world without any freedom at all

it is better than a puppet world that cannot go astray

might it be the best of all worlds possible
within the limits of free exercise of will
better than a world lacking freedom to be tested
better than a world not required to seek virtue through
      self-control
a better world than any of its alternatives lacking choice
with its hazards
yet with finite freedom to grow in response to grace

your will gave us the best of all possible worlds
despite the wrath of our bad willing

these limits constitute the actual world
in which we are required to go on voyages of trial
meet challenges never thought manageable
thus grow or wane in virtue

you made this world better than I ever could have imagined
had I the power

though pride still tempts me to think
I could have done better

Mid-morning—Third Hour (Terce)

I watch the wind

    I watch the wind toss flimsy leaves into the air
    swirling as if just to play with space
    bending the tops of towering trees
    to test their strength as winter comes

    some want to be as far from wind as possible
    I want to be near enough to feel its touch
    to let it caress my face

Noon—Sixth Hour (Sext)

no worthless moment

    this is no wasted day
    when accompanied by you

no moment worthless
if you attend
no sound so dissonant
no sight so ugly
that cannot be embraced
within the beauty of your holiness

Mid-afternoon — Ninth Hour (None)

a thousand blackbirds

> living as well now as I did with bare feet on prairie clay
> when nothing was amiss
> ready to take what comes
> provided for wholly

> with a thousand blackbirds in a single tree
> with one bull frog at water's edge
> with two white geese gently moving together
> in a straight slow line downstream
> again I come to you with joy
> lacking nothing I can think of

Evensong (Vespers)

remembering light

> amid the memory of a declining sun
> lost like a ghost on the far horizon
> I rest content
> with the unique privilege of embracing the darkness
> that comes as a subtle pledge of morning

Nighttime (Compline)

nothing without providence

> as night falls
> the breeze lifts the baked magnolia leaves
> brushing the feathers of the gull

> as the gold of the horizon reddens

the refractions of light from the lake
witness your splendor

nothing you offer is given senselessly
without divine forethought of creature's needs
nothing we endure is borne without providence

──────────────── **DAY 3** ────────────────

Before Dawn (Vigils)

a glimpse of the whole

> it takes the whole truth to ground a seed of faith
> to make the soul alive

> even with but a glimpse of truth
> the soul is fed by hope

First Hour of Morning (Lauds)

the web

> the spider's brilliant web shines in the sun
> bracing for the wind
> flowing as if in a gentle river of moving shapes
> the pattern unveils an inspired design
> fine as a feather
> tough enough for heavy wind
> engineered by a tiny creature

Mid-morning—Third Hour (Terce)

the sudden entry of the pelican

> the white pelican sails in
> just above the waves
> spanning the length of the bend

> the sky is blue and my soul is warm and comforted
> geese swim safely midstream
> staying together in an intimate circle

Noon—Sixth Hour (Sext)

the disappearing mist

>   the spray booms high above the waves
>   the wind pulverizes the sheet of water into a disappearing
>   mist
>   synchronized with children's laughter

>   let me be as lithe as lifted spray
>   responsive to every breeze
>   ready to rise in the wind
>   give me weightlessness
>   even if for a moment

>   then I will seek lowliness
>   moving gently toward the sea

Mid-afternoon—Ninth Hour (None)

the sole beholder

>   you bless the sole beholder of this time and place
>   in this season so blessed
>   by warmth, leisure, beauty, fecundity

>   for all those named ones I've had on my heart today
>   I ask your blessing on each one
>   consecrating this day to your glory

Evensong (Vespers)

what if

>   I ask in fantasy
>   what if
>   as if the if were already there in palpable reality

>   when pure imagination becomes lost
>   from the native soil of here and now
>   freedom hangs bleeding on the cross of not yet
>   conjuring phantom sinews less durable

bones less firm than mine
opening the transom to glimpse despair

I have no time for despair
not even a moment
no reason for reckless introspection
no cause to lose my footing
not with a life encompassed by hope

Nighttime (Compline)

short-lived economy

what sort of economy is this
to spend liver and kidney
on short-lived folly
to yield to death with shortened days
a member that intends to be
the means to cleanse and fuel life

─────────────── DAY 4 ───────────────

Before Dawn (Vigils)

what God remembers

even if nothing in creation endures in time
you hold it easily in your eternal memory
for you it is effortless

for me it is hard
locked in finite time
where even the memory of the patriarchs fades
where death ends the memory of all things finite

but you know and remember all
all motives
all loves
all aspirations
all hopes
all choices

however trivial
they are all remembered, embraced, redeemed

First Hour of Morning (Lauds)

begin with bread

> let the day begin with bread
> and end with wine
> letting time flow gently in between

> let the year begin with advent
> and end with kingdomtide
> letting time flow gently in between

> letting time itself be reclaimed for your glory

Mid-morning — Third Hour (Terce)

casting bread

> if but one in a thousand is edified
> the endeavor is justified
> so I plant apple seeds in moist soils

> I cast your living bread upon capricious waters
> leaving it to you with hidden currents
> to give birth and nurture

Noon — Sixth Hour (Sext)

a perfect moment

> a perfect moment to be perfect
> must be eternal
> all imperfections dwell in time

> yet here in this bright clean air
> the moment seems virtually unimprovable

> let me breathe it deep
> with nothing added
> with no attempt at multiplication

Mid-afternoon — Ninth Hour (None)

the front arrives suddenly

> from the distant hill comes first the whisper of the
>   wind
> the fever in the air disappears suddenly
> the winds sweep in as warning
> then blowing light coverlets of rain on the waves
> then heavy poundings
> blanketing the valley

> lightning breaking through dark clouds
> the heavens announcing an altered atmosphere

> never fear the rain
> only the long absence of rain
> be awed by the gift required for survival
> do not whine when all is wet
> were it not wet it would not be giving life

Evensong (Vespers)

high above this earthly space

> high above this earthly space spreads the cosmos
> unimaginably deep beyond deep
> not merely all that is
> but more than all that is in passing time
> pointing to the one and only you who transcend time
>   and space

> the graying sky holds mysteries
> that do not yield to finite inspection
> untouched by time-bound reason

> every moment brings me a shade closer to twilight
> which opens softly with songs from trees
> with hymns from tiny insect choirs

Nighttime (Compline)

echoes

>   so now ends the day
>   so now echoes the softness of your word
>   so now shouts your silence
>   so now comes your fulfillment in time
>   so now may all behold your glory
>
>   stamp your seal upon my soul
>   embracing all uncertainty

───────────────── **DAY 5** ─────────────────

Before Dawn (Vigils)

deep waters

>   unfinished fragments of thoughts
>   invade my hours of darkness
>   plunging me into deep waters
>   where there is no floor
>   for crabs to hug

First Hour of Morning (Lauds)

what I most need

>   you invited me to ask
>   so now I ask
>   what I most need in this voyage
>
>   close bonding with the saints
>   historic witnesses to you
>   freedom and solitude
>   self-control and stability
>
>   time as needed to absorb your word
>   to rest at night
>   to breathe deeply without anxiety
>   that I may more fully refract your glory

despite enduring imperfections in my life, speech, and soul

the prayers of those who share my vocation

the trust of my family

this I ask of you
who asked me to ask

Mid-morning—Third Hour (Terce)

so flows the mystery

here seeds are sewn and little ones given birth
letting time flow through their living cells
made of multitudes of microscopic channels and energies
which they cannot see or know

so flows the mystery of the breeze
on the rocks by the lake in the winter sun

Noon—Sixth Hour (Sext)

psalms learned by heart

accompany me into those ancient hidden baptisteries
where new life arose from chilly waters
take me to places of retreat
where the spirit was poured out
the written word poured over
transmitted by common lay consent
through faithful generations
where psalms were learned by heart
to shape the daily rhythm of work and prayer
I search for Hippo where your servant Augustine labored
prayed, taught, and died
with vandals on the outskirts of the city

Mid-afternoon—Ninth Hour (None)

autumn's pledged to winter

the branches that once offered shade

now bare and pledged to winter
are ready for the wind
reaching for roots instead of sky

Evensong (Vespers)

night by night

the voice of mating rises in the evening
in hints of loneliness and reunion

the flicker of fireflies
the hoot of the owl
the chirping of the sparrows
the unbroken refrain of the cricket
the croaking frog
the gossip of the June bugs
all rise above the flow of the river

the territorial cry
marks boundaries for love
it happens night by night
under the weaving gestures of the tallest tree
over tiny ripples of the deepest stream

Nighttime (Compline)

let the debate about your justice end

let the debate about your justice end
let all things be received at once directly from your hand
let time be enveloped in eternity
let all who have breath glorify your name

now falls the night
now lifts the silent breeze
now flows the stream of time toward darkness
now you give breath and voice
now you enter my heart
now you review with me my conscience
now you find me wandering and bring me home

now you rightly claim dominion over all my inward motives
now you offer the inestimable gift of your presence
now you make good on all your promises of old
now you prove your unending faithfulness
now you share your life with me as I offer my life to you
now you are my sovereign Lord
known and beheld as source and end of all
you who alone are worthy of worship

DAY 6

Before Dawn (Vigils)

the half moon

> the half moon splits the sky
> blessing the night above the sleeping oaks

> I wander by the dark shore
> feet sinking into soft grass
> loving the illumined night

> we are made to love what is beautiful
> it would be unfitting to walk too quickly

First Hour of Morning (Lauds)

faith comes through facing loss

> only through challenges have I grown
> only when worked have muscles strengthened
> faith has come through facing loss
> through maladies survived
> apostasy confronted
> partings endured

Mid-morning—Third Hour (Terce)

uncommonly free

> compared with sellers and buyers in the vast market of duties
> I am uncommonly free

when finitude is made free by grace

after a lifetime of task-bearing I rejoice
in the gracious freedom lived out here and now
as long as I'm allowed
being neither overly equipped nor stingily supplied

Noon — Sixth Hour (Sext)

the limits of memory

notes borne of the moment
jotted on tiny slips and scraps and napkins
provide a record of my journey with you
without them I would remember too little of our
        meeting
or what you whispered in my heart

Mid-afternoon — Ninth Hour (None)

prairie sun

this is a prairie sun
wide and high above the harvest
that bears down upon the quiet day beside the cool
        stream
where imperial snow geese monitor the valley
where the red hawk perches high above the rabbit trails
under a sun that touches every leaf of the ancient
        willow tree
slender, beautiful, bendable with the wind

Evensong (Vespers)

slowing down

while the evening is peeling back thin layers of darkness
someone is going home with a tapping cane

the stately swimming of geese is slow
as they make their leisurely turn around the bend
my spirit moves with them in their unruffled gait

the goslings born in the willow trunk two weeks ago
each one a tiny ball of fur
now eagerly feed on grass and seed
soon will look like toddlers
a third as tall as their proud parents

they know they belong together
ready for the dark canopy
being pulled across the evening sky

in a day that moved too fast what could be more fitting
than to move slowly at their pace
relishing this time with you

Nighttime (Compline)

just dream

quit the late-night task
rest warm
dream in the normal way
without prompting
just dream in receipt of God's glory

———————————— **DAY 7** ————————————

Before Dawn (Vigils)

freely called

like a genetic stamp upon the bone
we are never so free as when bound
to the deepest calling within
even when its lofty blessings seem a curse
whether in parenting or politics
sales or song
meditating or debating
escaping or barely surviving
the faithful remain always called to fruitful joy
whatever the burdens

First Hour of Morning (Lauds)

the silent sound of resurrection

> with you the silent sound of resurrection
> echoes through far hills
> leaving linens folded in the tomb

> with you the morning sings
> the valley breathes
> the symphony continues hushed

> the slender light of sleeping dawn awakens
> pushing away shadows
> signaling the light
> no darkness can overcome
> no length of time outlive
> no army's might can conquer

> it dawns with such fragility
> growing steadily through the morn

Mid-morning — Third Hour (Terce)

already here in place

> after a long journey without a compass
> stepping out into the day
> hoping for a plan, a vision, an explanation
> I am surprised to find all things here in place
> already dwelling in my heart
> fulfilled and known and palpable

Noon — Sixth Hour (Sext)

the music of grace and freedom

> what is the midday breeze singing
> what ode is it reciting
> what glimpse of wisdom recollected
> what truth beheld

now see the way that grace courts freedom
how they mingle into one
how they love each other
how they belong together in intimate embrace
one with the other
not alone
no grace unreceived
no act without grace

Mid-afternoon — Ninth Hour (None)

the harvest of today

reaping the harvest of today
I taste the grape
crush the grain
store the increase
pay out the deficit
settle accounts
pray for forgiveness
hope for mercy

Evensong (Vespers)

let time dance

sound the copper horn
let the flute lift up the soul
launch a piercing note from the trumpet
let fly the feet
in tune with time
in balance with space
fill the flute with cheerful melody

now is the time
here is the space
lift up the chalice

Nighttime (Compline)

the Son who prays

would the Son who prays continually in heaven
that we be reconciled to the Father
be likely to destroy those forever
who are wholly relying on his promise

Interlude: Communion with Christ through Prayer

The whole of time is put in perspective through communion with Christ in the Eucharist. Each phase of time is being reshaped in the light of life in Christ, his coming, dying, and coming again. Then the next day: his descent to incarnate life, his death, his resurrection, his ascension, his promised return.

As the sequence of the day sets the natural background of the coming and going of light, the incarnate, dying, and risen Christ is met in each phase of the changing day.

Throughout the whole daily order of prayer Christ himself is praying for and through us. The Holy Spirit is crying out with and for us through the hours.

The whole worldwide community of believers works daily in ordinary vocations. When each one prays, so with the whole church throughout the whole world. They pray through Christ by the power of the Spirit throughout the day as deep as grace and freedom allow. Each receives the benefit of being prayed for by others — family, friends, and intercessors all over the world. All believers in their vocations are called to pray through the hours both with others and individually.

The ordering of time through prayer integrates the prayer of the ancient psalms into the daily life of believers today, expressing the meaning of each phase of night and day in its season. The ordered reading from the Word of God at each phase of night and day, as well as readings from classical Christian teachers, illumines the meaning of the mystery of God's presence with humanity. In the daily ordering of time the Word of God is so read and meditated upon that it itself becomes a prayer. In this way the daily ordering of time in the presence of God is like an extension of the eucharistic life into our vocations.

Each of the seven canonical hours is understood in the light of the coming in time of the incarnate Lord. Each hour in time is set in relation to the end of time. That end is viewed in relation to the consummating purpose of history revealed in the incarnation and resurrection. Each hour of night and day corresponds with scriptural memories of Christ's own life in time. His incomparable presence in time illumines our daily presence in time. He is born into our time. He embodies the coming reign of God. He dies for us. He redeems us from the netherworld. He rises from the grave to confirm the meaning of his earthly and timely ministry. Our times are seen in relation to his future coming.

By praying with the whole church throughout the hours of all the varied events of the day, whether sleeping, waking, working, relaxing, reading, celebrating, they all become an expression of the sanctification of time and place.

Meditating through the Hours with Scripture

Meditation through the hours means to live with scripture through the day, praying with the ancient church of apostolic times in a way that was primitively ordered in the Psalms. It has been offered as a gracious way of life for Christians.

Meditating through a sequence of hours is not unique to Christianity, but orthodox Christians have provided its most memorable form. This form has survived over two millennia. The faithful follow it not because they must but because they love it, and experience divine love through it. They love it because it gives them the joy of the presence of God on a sustained basis. It gives them deep grounding in the written word of scripture and the living Word of Jesus Christ. It brings to them a regular recollection of scripture's pattern of life with God by focusing on the Psalms.

The church does not meditate on the hours as such, but on God as revealed in scripture through the hours. To meditate through the hours is to inhabit the community of faith in time. It is to live within the world of the hopes and expectations of the people of Israel looking toward the coming of the Messiah, to pray with them the Psalms of the people of Israel. According to Christian experience these hopes became fulfilled in Jesus Christ. The messianic promises of the Psalms are at the center of the ordering of the hours. This is why praying through the hours is centered in Christ, who fulfills the promises. The faithful know that these promises have been fulfilled. For they know that their own lives have been already uplifted by the grace they offer. They themselves are made anew as proof of their fulfillment.

Sixth Week

DAY 1

Before Dawn (Vigils)

you than whom nothing greater can be conceived

> who are you who meets me at dawn?
> you are the only One than whom nothing greater can be
>   conceived
>
> Anselm got it centuries ago
> nothing greater can be conceived than you
> yet you meet me quietly at dawn
>
> you who must exist if rightly conceived
> who cannot be rightly conceived as if without existing
>
> if I imagine you as if you did not exist
> that image would not be you

First Hour of Morning (Lauds)

the artist of the firmament

> I have traced the stroke prints of the artist of the firmament
> repainting daily, hourly
> ever rearranging the scenery of time
> never tiring of perfecting light and shade anew
> the panorama always newly touched up each moment
>
> master painter of day and night
> from dawn to midnight
> you are forever exquisitely remaking
> what once looked nonimprovable
> yet succeeded then by another more perfect tint
> making anew all creation
> in the ever-changing red gold canyon of sky and sun

Mid-morning — Third Hour (Terce)

your fullness

> what could be more filling
> than being empty in your presence
> ready to receive

> what could be more empty
> than being without your fullness
> unable to give

Noon — Sixth Hour (Sext)

the heart desires to speak

> the heart desires to speak
> but only in its own heart language
> more by touch than words
> more as echo than sound

> the heart needs only time and space to speak

> to pour itself out in love quick to respond
> to answer without pretense

Mid-afternoon — Ninth Hour (None)

witness to your caring

> let me rightly hear your still small voice
> attest it truly without embellishment

> grant me full openness to now-unfolding time
> let me witness to your providing grace
> made known in creation, providence, history
> on the cross and in the giving of the Spirit

Evensong (Vespers)

architect of time

> architect of time and space
> incomparable artist of the sky
> designer of all that is

you paint the heavens now with radiant burgundy
against a soaring scenery of fiery light
draping billowing vapors high above the earth
lending your splendor to this remote place
unburdening my heaviness

Nighttime (Compline)

clinging to the evening

the birds are gone
absent, resting safely
the crickets have joined in the symphony of the
       evening
the dogs in the distance protect their turf
the bass are no longer striking
the tops of the trees are still as a statue
casting dark green patterns and subtle watermarks under
       the sky

all is at rest, ready for the descent of the night
without resistance or anxiety
it is time to retire
but I prefer to cling to the evening outdoors
where still unimaginable colors await
no one has the skill to paint such a scene
were I a photographer I could frame but not capture
       the serenity

—————————————— DAY 2 ——————————————

Before Dawn (Vigils)

swift and silent messages

the wind is blowing dizzily
through the night air
bearing its swift and silent messages
to and from the heart

First Hour of Morning (Lauds)

without distraction

> being with you in time
> is to be entirely without distraction
> to hear echoes of your Word made known
> in the cosmos you are creating
> redeeming and bringing to a fit conclusion

> being without distraction
> requires a very quiet time
> some completely cleared space
> to let the echo of your anvil be heard
> even if faintly
> ringing here and now

Mid-morning — Third Hour (Terce)

an unknown way

> my calling is to trust in you
> to bring to fulfillment a cloudy destiny
> even when it seems absurd

> you call me to an unknown way
> to take an untried step
> into the dark of future time

Noon — Sixth Hour (Sext)

itinerary

> the present day's breath is faith's itinerary
> the singular full request of now its only attention
> the sight of yes its only beholding
> the moving scent of time its plan

Mid-afternoon — Ninth Hour (None)

time to remember

> the western clouds hold sway
> over a golden blue horizon

a day filled with blessings is circling down
nearly done
time to remember one by one
what happened in the cooling day
of rediscovered kinships

Evensong (Vespers)

settle my spirit

settle my spirit deep into your arms
guide my steps along the steep and risky way
refresh me with the showers of late evening

bless me with the glowing traces of the night
fading from gold to black
with unspeakable beauty

Nighttime (Compline)

scattered pieces of the puzzle

so many pieces of the puzzle of nature and history
I have glimpsed through a glass darkly
without seeing the whole
I trust on that last day I will see face to face

you have taught me
but I have learned unevenly
learned too much I still do not know
learned without taming the beast in me
learned widely but within the narrow frame of my conceits
glimpsed beauty without its splendor being fully savored

———————————— DAY 3 ————————————

Before Dawn (Vigils)

on the silent shore

where steep cliffs meet the frozen water
on the silent shore I ponder

how to be me
how I came to be
who named me
how tiny fluid embryonic cells
were shaped at length into my bones
how light and time were given me to grow
why someone was there to tend my needs
for food and love and shelter
stirred constantly with care

that I am here at all is a marvel

First Hour of Morning (Lauds)

without knowing

when the ancient patriarch left Ur
he found himself
by finding you in promise
without knowing where he might next be going

when the ancient patriarch left Canaan
he found himself
by finding you in promise
without knowing where he might next be going

when the ancient patriarch left Egypt
he found himself
by finding you in promise
without knowing where he might next be going

so I go now
not knowing where
sure of your call

Mid-morning—Third Hour (Terce)

cliffside

no gently sloping sand here
only steep rocks plunging in a roiling sea
the gulls wing high

the sun glows through white clouds
tempering the summer day
I sit high on a flat rock on a point
all I want is here

Noon — Sixth Hour (Sext)

the curling river

tomorrow today and yesterday blend
into the curling river

all time flows like a breeze
swift to who knows where
from where to where
no one can say
swept by the moving squall

every move is linked with every other move
nothing comes or goes of itself
all things know all things together
while knowing nothing alone

Mid-afternoon — Ninth Hour (None)

teach me to settle in

when my freedom despairs of its boundless possibilities
it reels with choices

harassed by no one but myself
I am doing what I have chosen to do
electing this from countless paths

teach me to settle with my own willing
under claims greater than my own will

Evensong (Vespers)

who visits me

who visits in the cusp of the evening
but you eternal source and end of life

who comes to call in this secluded cove
but you the judge judged in my place

your glory settles upon the shadows
under a sky that takes breath away

shall I complain
about the way you have entered my life
through that ungainly way of fleshly birth
shall I test you on why you died an ugly death
shall I quiz you on your resurrection
as if I had the right or wisdom
to put you on trial

Nighttime (Compline)

without a visible fingerprint

so ends the day
without fanfare
no trumpet blast
it is just over
that is all

yet in itself was perfect
complete as a particular day
without analogy

you visited without a visible fingerprint

―――――――――――――――― **DAY 4** ――――――――――――――――

Before Dawn (Vigils)

as night enters borrowed time

as day sinks into a warm spiral
as distant lights project a glowing patina on the
    waves
as the horizon dims
as night enters borrowed time
all things are yours

all things humbled before you
bowed low in your presence
anticipating the last day

First Hour of Morning (Lauds)

behold the reflection

you placed me in a real world with real freedom
then gave me freedom to pray for grace
to exercise my freedom rightly

bring your glory close by
overflow dry cups
out of the abundance of your eternal being
that we may behold the reflection
of your glory in time

Mid-morning—Third Hour (Terce)

the truth that never tires

after a full-orbed active life
I thirst for solitude

the noisy times are over
I put my shortening time to its better use
inhabiting the precincts of the saints
singing their canticles
sitting at the feet of devout teachers of the sacred
text
bearing witness to the truth
that ever again asks to be beheld in time
sung, studied, and sought
the truth that never tires either mind or body
enlivening the soul

what could be a more fitting summit
to an active life

Noon — Sixth Hour (Sext)

would anyone

> if my eternal life is gained by your self-offering
> would you then
> turn away from my plea
> precisely when I am full of confidence in your word
>> clearly promised

> wouldn't it be absurd for me to turn away
> from my own eternal life
> just at the time when I have most reason
> to trust the one who offers it

> ask yourself
> would you
> would anyone?

> so embrace with confidence
> his word promised
> his offering nailed

Mid-afternoon — Ninth Hour (None)

receiving time

> no one can take away
> what time calls now
> it only goes on birthing another now
> to be received again in wonder
> swimming slowly like the foot stroke of the swan

> all we are given is a small taste of now
> a tiny slice
> which is never seized as if possessed
> only received as given

> to seize the day is a counsel of despair
> better simply receive the day
> holding it close to the bosom gently
> not tightly

Evensong (Vespers)

close the book

> set the manuscript aside
> listen to the silent disappearance of the turtle
> open my eyes to what is there
> in the sunset

> close the book
> look intently at what perfectly is
> smell the evening's cedar smoke

Nighttime (Compline)

I'd best not know

> when I ask about the whence and whither of my life
> much about the answer I need not know
> cannot ever know
> had best not know
> since my weak vision would distort it

> for this reason your purpose lies hidden
> opaque in the darkening dusk
> until at last revealed

Interlude: The Hours Viewed Classically

Athanasius, Basil, Augustine, and Benedict are the major classic Christian writers honored by global Christians of all cultures who have taught believers how to order time. They are frequently quoted by Protestants, Orthodox, and Catholics as reliable biblical interpreters, and have been esteemed for fifteen centuries.

These four teachers remain crucial resources of the Protestant patrimony as well, whether one is Presbyterian or Pentecostal. Since the most respected evangelical teachers like Luther and Calvin and Wesley make frequent and venerated reference to these and other church fathers, they are available to modern believers as thoughtful scriptural interpreters.

Scripture teaches and expects believers to pray. The practice of ordered daily prayer is not alien to Protestantism. I was taught in Sunday school as a child to pray upon rising, pray before breakfast, lunch, and dinner, then gather with the family for scripture reading in the evening accompanied by prayer; and pray at my bedside. This is the slender Protestant residue of the ancient practice of the hours, but its core is sustained. Seven times a day I learned to pray as a kid.

The discipline of praying through the seven set-apart times of the day, as did the psalmist, can still serve Protestants and charismatics as well as Catholics and Orthodox as a guide for daily prayer. The ordered hours offer a means to sanctify the entire day's activity without idolatry or legalism. They enhance and intensify meditation on the living Word of God in scripture.

Evangelical and Orthodox

I am unapologetically an evangelical who affirms with Orthodox and Catholic Christians the authority of scripture, the sole Lordship of Jesus Christ, and the call to live life in God through the Spirit. I am among those people that academics are prone to misname *fundamentalism* because they are so unacquainted with the actual history of fundamentalism.

I am braced for criticism from Catholics who may think this is too evangelical or pietistic, and from evangelicals who may feel this effort is too Catholic or traditional. My answer: the practice of praying through the hours is small-c catholic without needing to be channeled through formal Roman canonical rules. It is a worldwide Christian practice without ceasing to be evangelical. It is derived from ancient Christian teaching, but not exclusively Western or Latin Christian teaching. It does not lose sight of the Eastern and African roots of pre-European Christianity. This is the intellectual ethos from which these meditations come.

I spent more than three decades of my professional life teaching graduate students in a celebrated university just outside of New York City with a well-furnished library where advanced students came hungering to discover the texts of ancient ecumenical Christianity — some Catholic, some Orthodox, some evangelical, some none of the above. These meditations hope to signal to evangelicals that this exercise of the hours is not at all primarily or exclusively Western Catholic but thoroughly scriptural. Catholic readers will find that this personalized treatment of the hours is broadly catholic even if not adherent to all the premises and rules of Western canon law, yet respectful of canon law viewed in the light of scripture.

Every essential feature of the canonical hours is ecumenical — ancient ecumenical — in ways that believing Protestants, Orthodox, and Catholics can affirm without a sacrifice of intellect. It is a structure of prayer that existed long before the late medieval scholastic sacramental dogma (the doctrine that observance of the sacraments is necessary for salvation and that such participation can of itself confer grace), which due to its abuses was aptly resisted by Luther, Calvin, Cranmer, and Wesley. It is an arrangement of the life of prayer that the Reformers themselves all practiced in some form, not as a legal requirement but as a gift of grace received.

The Hours for Protestants

Believers love to study the written Word. They do not need some external incentive besides scripture to pray through the hours. To pray through the hours is to pray out of scripture and thus to come closer to scripture, not more distanced from it. The Psalms and scripture texts that form the textual core of the liturgy of the hours are canonical texts for all believers. The hours are largely a rehearsal of scripture treated meditatively through the phases of time.

The hours of prayer have been a feature of Jewish and Christian worship for centuries of biblical preaching. In the modern period they have three families of memory and interpretation: Eastern Orthodox, Western Catholic, and globally evangelical Protestant. My own tradition is derived from the Anglican form of the liturgy of the hours. When Wesley rose at 4:15 a.m. every morning, he was deliberately following the habit of the early Christians who rose early for Matins. It is not alien to me as a Protestant in the tradition of Calvin and Hooker and Wesley to recognize, as an aspect of my baptism, the commitment to pray constantly with the church of all times and places.

—————— DAY 5 ——————

Before Dawn (Vigils)

pink wide dawn

> light awakens
> spreading over an adagio sky
> pink white pastels brighten
> as they kiss deep waves
> the symphony unfolds
> through a thousand shades of orange and blue

First Hour of Morning (Lauds)

inhabited

> the cove is well inhabited
> despite its seeming quietness
> by creatures of great ingenuity and beauty
> the heron's great wingspan gently glides over windswept water
> the squirrel leaps tree to tree
> the pintails bob safely on rocky waves
> the mallards feed on shore then scurry toward the safe center of
> the lake
> a thousand blackbirds take possession of a single tree
> while far away a lone carpenter shingles a roof
> the early morning hammer blows echo through the trees
>
> open my eyes to gifts hidden in the morning air

Mid-morning—Third Hour (Terce)

in search of solitude

> let it go away
> the corrupting social scene
> packed and sweaty

let it disappear from my view
let it yield to nature and the love of learning
leave me alone a while
with quiet praise and honest confession
let me be free from being scheduled for anything at all
give me time to come to you
commune with you
receive your blessing

Noon—Sixth Hour (Sext)

the complaint of my conscience against me

I am playing meaningless games
where no one knows the score

who cares what's in my head
unless it bears fruit for another

better just do what is at hand
even if the will is weak

Mid-afternoon—Ninth Hour (None)

come again tomorrow

you who came yesterday
come again tomorrow
you who convoyed me through those rough seas
remain with me to my destination

I would stumble if you did not admonish
I could not endure a moment but for you sustaining me

do not let me roam without a compass
do not leave me to my own devices

Evensong (Vespers)

settle my soul

settle my soul after a pressing day
that I may hear your hushed word at twilight

behold your glory in the vanishing dusk

you who grant the peace of the nightfall
the soft colors, the fading light
the shadows, the deepening greens of distant trees
the easy drift of leisurely water
touched by a gentle breeze

acquaint me with myself
with who I am just now
bowing to your glory

Nighttime (Compline)

so where did the past go

what happened to what was
where did it go
how did it disappear
who took it
why did it go away
when will it return
where will it be when found

nothing happened
really it went nowhere
having no place to stand
no time left to fix itself into an ornament
leaving no measurable entity

this is where time goes
nowhere
forever received by eternity

—————————————— **DAY 6** ——————————————

Before Dawn (Vigils)

hurricane

a hurricane of images still streams through my brain
washing away walls thought secure

faster than I can swim or sprint
sweeping through today as if there were no yesterday
striking swiftly
as if upon Job's children
swirling around all rational planning or reasoning
taking with it good and evil

give me patience to rebuild
even if not to grasp its eventual meaning
in the tangled threads of providence
pointing toward the last day

First Hour of Morning (Lauds)

the aging willow

in a favored place by water's edge
the aging willow with split and crooked trunks
still attempts to breathe the sun
drink the edges of the shore
bend with every breeze

many winters have passed
since they said
too many storms rode on heavy winds
too many broken limbs
too many insects hungry to feed
too many hazards
too much decay

years ago the experts pronounced it dead

my hunch is that it will outlast me
happily for this valley

Mid-morning — Third Hour (Terce)

why life still burns

I've wondered
why does life still burn in my brief candle

the faithful have traveled so far through the desert
stored so much in memory
only to see memory fail
all recollection lost

to write this down
to etch it in hard stone
this is why life still burns in my brief candle

Noon — Sixth Hour (Sext)

even nothing points to you

all that we call nothing
is what is absent from you who fully are

your incomparable way of being is fuller than any way I can
conceive of you

all that can be called "netherworld" means only this —
to be distanced forever from you who fully are
from you than whom nothing greater can be conceived

when terror tests the air, remember
the nothing of the anxiety that for a moment so seems to be
comes finally to nothing
so that even the nothing points toward you who
make and remake all that is

Mid-afternoon — Ninth Hour (None)

when peace comes

peace comes into my soul

when I see fine mists refracting colored light
uplifted by an unexpected breeze

when I hear the gentle near-silent croak
of a snow white egret winging homeward

when my feet feel sand on a quiet beach
alone with my closest companions

both alive and gone

then my heart leaps up and settles in my soul
at some unfathomable depth

Evensong (Vespers)

a dot light years away

a tiny star appears amid descending light
the first witness of the night
to your immeasurable glory
how cheerfully it accompanies the glow of evening
defying the setting sun

assured of its lengthy path through time
the evening star appears early

here am I light years away
from that tiny beacon in the sky
which you have summoned into view

far from being made smaller by the vast extent of
        space
I am lifted up by it
for you have given me the modest power of recognition
illumined its unimaginable distance in time
I am blessed by a strange closeness
to the visual linkage you allow
to distant space through rolling darkness

Nighttime (Compline)

welling up from within

an unspoken word
welling up from within
unexpectedly claims my soul
hungering for fuller expression
then urgently requires eviction from silence

if I had a wish it would be this

nothing more
no wisdom, no relevance
just here and now speech
flung from the heart toward unfilled time

DAY 7

Before Dawn (Vigils)

the flood

a heavy black muddy burial
you have permitted it
to inundate all they valued in the world

when will the dying have time to learn from it
when will they know its meaning
the destruction is too absurd
too sudden to carry anything away
how could such devastation be wrought
on those for whom you died

only you can show what good can come from evil
and that only in due time

you have promised to show us how
a hard reckoning might wedge open
the stuck door of repentance

First Hour of Morning (Lauds)

clipping words

the barber cuts hair
as I clip phrases
trimming them down
to truth now pruned
to better size and symmetry

Mid-morning—Third Hour (Terce)

long days ahead

> ten days abroad takes more energy than it seems I have
> obsessively thinking ahead on unseen contingencies
> deciding, arranging, imagining
> it takes hard work before, during, and after
>
> what one sees as a privilege
> another feels as a burden
>
> I pray for a patient spirit
> openness to your guidance
> for courage through lengthening days

Noon—Sixth Hour (Sext)

the state of things just now

> in the warming sun the geese appear
> clad in black and brown and white
> to parade in front of tall trees
> while locusts begin to sing
> a hawk surveys the valley from a tree top
>
> keep me on track in steady pace
> through midday into the evening
> to be strong for tomorrow's gifts and tasks

Mid-afternoon—Ninth Hour (None)

when I listen to myself

> fatigue drags on
> but breath continues
> the voice creaks
> but thoughts abound
> nerves tremor
> but the will remains focused
> cold winds blow over me
> they pierce my soul

the day is long and gone
the night arrives in welcomed time

six days of creation are complete
the time has come to rest

Evensong (Vespers)

the dust-laden bouquet of fallen leaves

    still clinging to their twigs
    not yet drifting down
    the air is full of the dusty sweet decay of yellowing
          leaves
    gliding down and floating away
    not knowing what to expect from wind or wave
    but yielded

    help me Lord to be so yielded
    ready for an unknown outcome
    like a leaf in late autumn
    disposed to meld with earth
    awaiting a new life
    ready for whatever you provide
    in the dampening night

Nighttime (Compline)

on this day I made choices

    it is I who did it
    made real choices on this day
    likely to shape another's future days
    choices never to be revoked
    with which I must forever live for good or ill

    now pleading for your clemency, Lord
    hoping for your redemption of what I cannot see
    bless those who may unintentionally suffer
    from my decisions without my intent

praying in advance for mercy upon unseen
    consequences
impossible to guess with my blurred senses
that dwell in the dusk between day and night

Interlude: Praying through the Hours in Early Christianity

The early church recognized in the Psalms the model form of prayer. They did not try to improve upon the Psalms, but to highlight them for Christian worship. Meditation on specific psalms constituted the central textual feature of the liturgy of the hours.

Long before the Benedictine movement the Psalms were already the central focus of daily meditation. Athanasius wrote to Marcellinus of the special value of the Psalms for Christian formation: "The Psalter has a very special grace ... Within it are represented and portrayed in all their great variety the movements of the human soul. It is like a picture in which you see yourself portrayed and, seeing, may understand and consequently form yourself upon the pattern given. You find depicted in it all the movements of your soul, all its changes, its ups and downs, its failures and recoveries.... Each of us sings the Psalms as though they had been written for our special benefit. We take and recite them, not as though someone else were speaking or another person's feelings were being described, but as if we were speaking of ourselves, offering the words to God as our own heart's utterance ... Before [the Lord] came among us, he sketched the likeness of this perfect life for us in the Book of Psalms" (Benedictine Daily Prayer, 1872–73).

As Christianity gradually separated from Judaism, the ancient practice of singing the Psalms through the hours continued. The central textual content of meditation from the outset has always been the Psalms (as suggested in Acts 4:23–30). Praying regularly the Lord's Prayer was also a standard practice, as indicated by the first known manual of Christian practice, the Didache (8.2–3, late first century). The First Letter of

Clement (40.1–4) confirms that by the second generation of apostolic witness, believers were praying at set times of the day.

This practice stood in direct continuity with Jewish practice of prescribed times of synagogue and temple prayer. The common early Christian practice was to pray on the first hour of daylight with the rising of the sun, and at the last hour of the day when the lamp was being lit. The sun, a symbol of Christ, provided light for morning prayer. The lamp was also a symbol of Christ, and provided light for evening prayer.

After 70 AD, both Jews and Christians were increasingly scattered across the Greco-Roman world in a dispersal known as the Diaspora. Diverse patterns evolved for the celebration of time in different ancient church provinces. In earlier decades praying through the hours occurred in house churches. Later it became more regulated by church authority. What is certain from the outset is that accepting baptism involved a believer's solemn commitment to daily prayer that implied constant responsiveness to God.

As Christianity spread, so too did the practice of the cycle of daily prayer. By the second and third centuries the most widely respected early biblical commentators — Clement (c. 150–215 AD), Origen (c. 185–254), Tertullian (c. 160–225) — assumed as normative the observance of prayers in the morning and at night as well as the so-called "little hours" of Terce, Sext, and None (Tertullian, *On Prayer*, 25). These were seen by the fathers as foreshadowed in the Psalms and Acts of the Apostles. These daily prayers could be observed individually, by families, or in public common worship.

The exhortation to rise from bed to pray in the middle of the night expressed the call to be always vigilant against the adversary and ready for the Lord's return (1 Pet. 5:8; Eph. 5:14). The ancient Eucharist services often followed a pre-eucharistic nocturnal "watch" or "vigil" prior to the actual Sunday celebration. In accord with the great respect paid to the Lord's Day and the previous Jewish custom of reckoning days from sunset to sunset, this service of preparation consisted largely of scripture readings and psalms.

The vigil stood in relation to Sunday as Advent stood in relation to Christmas. It was an act celebrating the expectation of God's coming. These vigils became a part of the daily round of prayer later known as the Liturgy of the Hours, or Daily Office.

The Call to Constancy

The daily ordering of timely prayer seeks to follow the New Testament command to "pray always" (Eph. 6:18; Col. 4:2). The whole course of day and night is made holy by the praise of God. By engaging in this daily order, the faithful embody the royal priesthood of all who are baptized.

By the fourth century, the desert fathers and mothers (the earliest monks and nuns) were looking for ways of living out St. Paul's command to "pray without ceasing" (1 Thessalonians 5:17 ESV). John Cassian reported that the early religious orders of Bethlehem were meeting together for prayer seven times in the course of the day to help them better to fulfill the biblical command to pray without ceasing (Rom. 1:9-10).

Attempts were made to obey the command literally. One group would read psalms and pray for one period and pass along the act of praying seamlessly to another group waiting to read and pray the next group of psalms. This provided a continuous cascade of intercession before the throne of God. Some went through the entire 150 psalms regularly. Eventually that was abandoned for a weekly cycle built around certain hours of the day. This was then shifted to a regularized cycle of psalms. This cycle appears today in the core readings of the liturgy of the hours.

Regardless of whether or not the fixed-hour prayers were said alone or in community, they were never thought to be individualistic in nature. Rather, they employed time-tested prayers of a worshiping community. Many believers felt called to memorize all of the Psalms. Those who could not read could memorize, assisted by singing the Psalms. They became the lively basis of personal reflection and meditation, not static or rote words.

Many Catholics today follow an official or magisterial form of prayer approved by the church for each step of the day. Protestants are more likely to meditate on scripture and pray freely by the power of the Spirit from the heart.

This collection of meditations stands deliberately in the Protestant tradition of Spirit-led prayer, deeply respecting the Catholic tradition of ordered prayer.

Anthony's life became the primary generating force behind many experiments in the ordering of time around the life of prayer. From his cave poured forth many different ascetic movements stretching from the Nile Valley to the Judean desert, the Syrian mountains, Cappadocian rivers, and all along the North African coastal plains and mountains.

All these were firmly in place in Africa and Asia before this ascetic (disciplined, athletic) way of ordering time became later firmly implanted in Europe following the time of John Cassian at Lérins, Benedict at Monte Cassino, and Patrick of Ireland. In the sixth century these three and their followers took the desert wisdom and transmitted it to the Latin West and Gaelic Ireland. Benedict's specific *Rules* for the ordering of time were taken largely from those described by John Cassian, in his *Conferences* and *Institutes*. These rules and sayings recalled through stories and sayings the desert monastic practices of the Nile and the Greek and Syriac East. Thus the Western form of the hours predates Benedict. He received them from the African desert fathers and mothers whose sayings and lives have inspired the life of prayer ever since.

Of the Western forms of the liturgy of the hours, the chief one to survive largely intact has been the Benedictine. It was in 525 that St. Benedict (480–543 AD) wrote the prototype Western manual for praying the Hours. The Rule of St. Benedict defined this pattern for the West. It combined earlier African and Palestinian practices with the Western daily office. This daily practice has from early times been believed by both Eastern and Western interpreters to have been passed down through the centuries from the apostles. The evidence is embedded in the Book of Acts itself.

Seventh Week

—————— DAY 1 ——————

Before Dawn (Vigils)

where will this day take me

> where will this day take me
> through what eddies will its rivers rush
> where will time deposit me tomorrow
> in what uncharted zone
>
> whatever the outcome
> your providence is sure

First Hour of Morning (Lauds)

to know as I am known

> I want to know myself
> as I am
> truly am
>
> to know myself
> as I am more truly known by you
> even if in part through a glass darkly
>
> I want to know you as you are
> in your timeless way
> so far as I am able
>
> remove the blinders from my eyes

Mid-morning—Third Hour (Terce)

the blessings of repentance

> set right my heart
> to lift up hands to you
> who stamped them with your image

let all corruptions poised to rot or rule
be washed away completely
allowing no ill will to cling

pardoned let me lift my face
without shame or scar
secure and fearless
misery forgotten
remembered only as waters long passed

then let my life glisten brightly as at noon
let darkness fade away as if in the high morning
with sure confidence grounded in hope
let me lie down and not be afraid
resting safely under firm shelter
where careworn souls come to seek your blessing

Noon — Sixth Hour (Sext)

dazed and stumbling

hard stricken midway through this daily warfare by
heavy blows
I look for something fixed to hold on to
dazed and stumbling forward
asking my feet to tell me where they are

hit hard I find I am still alive
clinging to my feet
looking for the real world

only then do I hear the closing bell
in a grueling round of a heavy day
now done

Mid-afternoon — Ninth Hour (None)

this encumbered flesh

how unprepared this flesh
to meet unseen tomorrows
so I dodge an accounting

I dally
evade as if I had forever to make amends

this encumbered flesh is not well made
to weather all potential hazards

with wounded conscience
I feel heavily the costs to others of my own free acts
aware that on the last day the testing will be fiery
if not covered by your mercy

it seems I hear already the last-round trumpet
poised to sound

Evensong (Vespers)

dampen the adrenalin fires

dampen the adrenalin fires
plunge me deep into the cool of evening
that I may feel the reaches of time's mystery
that I may emerge more fit
for the pure light of eternity

Nighttime (Compline)

shape my spirit

shape my spirit
form it in your image
mold my heart and tongue
let my voice be an instrument of your glory and goodness
burn away the hubris
do not let it take root

—————————————— **DAY 2** ——————————————

Before Dawn (Vigils)

but for the mind of God

the dawn unhurried
searches out glimmering waves

to serve as mirrors of your rising glory
while darkness yields to morning

as the sky's tints overflow and flood
phasing in and out like water colors
let the high dam of vivid pigments
break upon the day

each moment of such a scene is to be beheld only once
then gone forever
but for the mind of God

First Hour of Morning (Lauds)

what more could I ask

I watch the waves stream by my deck
without task or time
without crew or schedule
in an unfettered life
as much as I can dream of
spared of hunger, pain, or dread
no pressing bonds except to the sky and sea and wind
        and gull
on a vast sea
under a pitiless taunting wind
what more could I ask
right here is where I want to be
where all the pieces come together

Mid-morning—Third Hour (Terce)

between skull and neck

it is between my neck and skull
throbbing with each heartbeat
this is my thorn

unwelcome but sending a repeated urgent communiqué
inviting me to slacken rein
relax grip

Noon—Sixth Hour (Sext)

whatever good I think I do

> whatever good I think I do
> finds its own way of becoming undone
> turned to spoilage
> lost from memory
> taken captive in battle
> brought to nothing
>
> even the best motives and actions
> infinitely distortable

Mid-afternoon—Ninth Hour (None)

having lost my balance

> having lost my balance
> fallen back into the quicksand
> I cry for help
> not that I deserved it
> but your extended hand is outstretched as promised
> if you are willing
> let me clutch it gratefully

Evensong (Vespers)

the chalice invites tasting

> the chalice invites tasting
> the plate offers living bread
> the living word brings low all pride
> raising spirits high
> celebrating the end of arduous battle
> rehearsing final victory
> savoring the crushed grape
> the taste of living bread
>
> I bathe in the fragrance of the feast
> with gentle talk of steadfast covenant love

having made peace with eternity
this is how you have taught me
to plunge into the depths of now

Nighttime (Compline)

so what

so what if I talk with myself now and then
mostly in late evening
when I stub my toe
or cannot find a lost letter
or fail to solve a simple equation
then I talk unembarrassed
being alone and unafraid of censure

yet not really alone
since always with you

———————————— **DAY 3** ————————————

Before Dawn (Vigils)

the coming banquet

let me glory in your unfettered way of seeing time
flow gently with the swells and breezes of your grace
glimpse some passing bit of your lengthy purpose in time
that you envisioned from before time
able to see all time now

let me bear the cup at the morning banquet
join the circle of the beloved faithful
singing along with every language the Holy Spirit speaks

wherever your gentle breeze appears
let me be ready to be moved by it
when you at last come in radiant light and cloud
let my eyes be open

First Hour of Morning (Lauds)

from the depths you have dredged my soul

> my imagination has flown too high
> over that of which I remained ignorant
> now settled in the sea

> from the depths you have dredged my soul
> lain so long in the bottom of the mire
> I have awaited your coming
> barely glimpsed what you have always known fully

> so now I bask in your light
> let my song accompany the sun to its height
> and radiate its glory

Mid-morning—Third Hour (Terce)

you walked with me

> you who met me on the icy mountain slope
> who walked with me near perilous crevices
> blessed me with your presence through the cold
>   night
> talked with me when I was not listening
> joined me when I thought I could go alone

> still you visit me
> despite my distant ways
> despite the far-off travels when we lost touch
> despite the fury of my will
> despite my absentminded wandering
> you have not let me stay as prodigal
> as I would have once willed myself to be

> I have been to far-away places
> where I deliberately willed to go and did go

> but never without you
> who ran to meet me upon my return

Noon—Sixth Hour (Sext)

the ice is melting

> the ice is slowly melting under midday sun
> disappearing into moving streams

> once they chipped fishing holes in the hard ice
> now it has changed to pliable liquid
> yielding to the pebble thrown
> bearing up a floating feather
> flowing down the valley

> so let my cold heart melt under your midday sun
> as it floats toward the sea

Mid-afternoon—Ninth Hour (None)

the broken vase

> my whole heart cracks and breaks
> like a fragile antique vase
> what once was whole now lies broken
> shattered on the floor

> we expected the ancient vessel to survive for
> generations
> never thought it vulnerable
> the missile came suddenly from nowhere
> no one saw it coming

> how do I pick up pieces I cannot even see
> restore my heart to the splendor once given

Evensong (Vespers)

being with you

> when all I hope for is already present
> I know instinctively what now means
> I have no explanation for the hidden causes
> only awareness of the gift

this is no time for pretending
for getting ready or cleaning up or storing
harvesting or planting

that is all done
it is time to attend the feast
it is now the eighth day
the time to rest free
to be
to be me
to be me here and now
in your presence

how I have striven during my life
worked, planned, struggled, fought
all worthwhile
but now I need do none of that
for the time being
just being with you

Nighttime (Compline)

at midnight they were found praying

> at midnight they were found praying
> Paul and Silas
> in prison
>
> now on this rocky cove I pray late with Paul and
> Silas
> for the prisoners in this valley
> that their chains may be broken

DAY 4

Before Dawn (Vigils)

from nowhere

> from nowhere to seeming nowhere
> you have taken me

my absurdity yielded to your guidance

now I arrive somewhere otherwise unthinkable
brighter with hope than ever I could have
imagined

First Hour of Morning (Lauds)

the terrain of an emerging day

the sloping terrain of a new day lies open
under the unbolted sky
with no hard plan to pursue
no fantasies to chase
no tight timetable to mind
no urgent goals to reach
no weighty musts or oughts

permit me grace to receive through the day this
freedom
the morning for the eye's delight
the evening for breathing mystery
the night for coming home

Mid-morning—Third Hour (Terce)

the voices of the wind

so what am I to do with you
windy spirit of the plain
in what accents do you speak this morning
entering invisibly
unexpectedly rising and falling
shifting and then still

the wind speaks in many voices
now whispering
now shouting
now splintering
then full of gentle caresses

Noon — Sixth Hour (Sext)

the pit of the deep canyon

> I never saw the hazard
> never considered any peril
> only wondered if I might be strolling
> a little near the ledge

> how did it happen that I slipped and fell
> into the lower depths of a deep canyon
> how with all the advantages
> how did it happen that I lost my footing
> wound up where I do not belong

> you permitted it to happen that I might learn
> how hazardous it is to be free

Mid-afternoon — Ninth Hour (None)

thirsting for truthful speech

> the command is clear
> the scales precise
> time for full confession
> uncovered now without deception
> acts that caused hurt
> deeds done thoughtlessly
> moments to regret
> careless words spoken brusquely

> my tongue thirsts for truthful speech
> burns open from the heart

Evensong (Vespers)

a time for just being

> condensed in this sundown blush
> are remnants of light gathered from the whole sky
> the valley glows in concentrated radiance
> the noon beheld in soft light

here and now there is no such thing as accomplishment
only being
no movement toward targets
only breathing
no steps to take
nothing to do
nothing to have or need
only be

exploits are hardly fitting for a moment like this

Nighttime (Compline)

rest deep now

time to give way
yield the entire field of action
take thoughts and dreams to ease
rest with sabbath blessedness
become buried to the day just gone
coming alive to hope alone

―――――――――――――― **DAY 5** ――――――――――――――

Before Dawn (Vigils)

disappearing

she appears in my dreams unexpectedly
in the background of a silent street
only to disappear without a word

there she is
but for a moment
she recognizes me and I her
yet before I speak she is gone
and I remain alone

grateful for an unexpected visit
grant me patience for our coming reunion

First Hour of Morning (Lauds)

the unwelcome companion of being free

> my hands are bound by the devices of my very hands
> my own freedom knots my own freedom
> in bindings that bind me only to myself
> in dormant guilt and anxiety
> that may reach out toward a third or fourth generation

> when I exercise my freedom I act with risk
> even when I do not choose I risk the upshot of not choosing

> rational creatures are free to choose
> but not free from the consequences of their choices
> human freedom dwells only within these finite limits
> the unwelcome companion of being free
> is to be bound by one's own choices

> the remedy is repentance
> hard but sure

Mid-morning — Third Hour (Terce)

finding all I've sought

> what could be better than to live an honest life by grace
> what could be more in harmony with myself
> than to be exactly who I am in speech and thought
> corresponding fully with this here
> this now
> merely to listen well and speak clearly
> nothing more
> nothing complex
> nothing on display but the true voice of time's unfolding
> being found by all I've sought

Noon — Sixth Hour (Sext)

beyond the range of my calling

> a hard but necessary learning for me
> to avoid unnecessary new adventures

so let imaginary journeys remain undone
let them sleep softly beyond the horizon of my calling

after a life of activity
what I now try to learn
how to do almost nothing
taking lessons in silence
content with what is given
not searching always for new fields to plant or harvest
not yearning for new exploits
but simply receiving
the breath, bread, blood, and time you've given

Mid-afternoon — Ninth Hour (None)

change me

when I prefer my fantasy to all others' reality
when I take more seriously myself than all the rest together
when I indulge my own passions with idealized excuses
sometime to others' harm without conscience or hesitation
I pray
change me thoroughly
remake my spirit
from the center out
like dropping a pebble in a silent pond
spreading from the center to every concentric ripple

Evensong (Vespers)

after all these years

after all these years of travail in toil
temptation and imagined terror
who could have guessed
my life would have come to rest in this pleasant place

the sun is showering the lapping waves with radiance
in an infinite number of unexpected angles
that glow

streaming through time
in that unusual order that befits the wind

Nighttime (Compline)

how you woo the beloved

through the narrow fissure of the fragile moment
the only way to move from past to future is to decide

through that tiny aperture you move deftly
to woo the imagination through reason to will fitly

through dark ambivalence you lead silently
by unseen hedging
without coercion
by gentle persuasion
without forcing

with purpose through my blinded time you lead
from that which was to that which is not yet

for this you Lord were born in time
to send your Spirit to fulfill the time

this is how you woo the beloved

—————————————— **DAY 6** ——————————————

Before Dawn (Vigils)

rise early

I rise early to watch the jonquils grow
to see the fins of fish appear for half a glance
I hardly have time to glimpse them
but you know each one uniquely

let the day commence
make taut the pulley
lift up the spirit
ride with the surge
shape the steel on the anvil

flatten it
put it in the fire to melt

let the match begin
let the marksman be ready
time is short
eternity longer than long

First Hour of Morning (Lauds)

an echo of your disappearance

> if you disappear for a while
> impart an echo of your disappearance
> if you tread softly away
> leave a footprint
> an aroma of your gentleness
> a ricochet through far hills
> of your strong voice

Mid-morning—Third Hour (Terce)

when nothing works

> on days when nothing works
> all attempts thwarted
> all first steps stumble
> give me courage to start anew
> as you started anew in human history
> in nativity and resurrection

Noon—Sixth Hour (Sext)

your glory she reflected

> I plead for her return
> come back
> be my companion in the winter
> weep with me when I weep
> dance with me in the whispered rhythms of the
> > evening

pray for me when I struggle
forgive when I go astray
stay with me on the long path

but she is gone
I live without her

with you Lord I am empowered to live without her
it is hard
yet made lighter by your grace

Mid-afternoon — Ninth Hour (None)

your mercy disarms

why do I grimace in your presence
like Adam caught with fruit peel in his teeth

why is my body unnerved
why do muscles twitch
why do I cough with a tight throat
why breathe with half a breath

because your glory overwhelms me
your holiness awes
your eternity makes fleeting all I know
your judging grace invades and exposes all inward
        obstacles
your embrace does not hold anything in reserve
your mercy disarms all defenses

Evensong (Vespers)

traces of a thousand colors

it is almost dark now
but the traces of a thousand colors cool the sky
now vanishing in the darkness
yet remaining in the mind
still tinting the horizon's retrospect

the wind is on the rise

making every remaining moment sweet before the
 storm
the summer dreams of lingering beyond its allotted
 time

let me savor the evening calm
as long as south winds let it last

Nighttime (Compline)

countless shapes of maybe

 discernment spins in a whirlpool
 with no predictable outcome
 whether life or death might follow remains unknown

 the rational mind is keenly aware of its vulnerability
 its exposure to time and heat and wind

 here swims uncertainty in countless shapes of maybe
 give me footing to survive

DAY 7

Before Dawn (Vigils)

all about nothing

 fears borne all night
 are all about nothing
 really nothing
 no substance to them
 spun purely out of imagination
 painting worst-case scenes in vivid detail

 why do I so fret about these things that are not in fact
  happening
 when faithful reasoning knows that none are dreadful
 none beyond your power to instruct me
 to learn by grace to cope with finitude
 no absolute threat lies buried in any of these imaginings
 nothing essential to my being

sure the heart will one day stop
the books will be sold
the store room cleaned up
the papers disposed of
this place will be lived in by others

so why do I fret
there is no good reason
literally all my worries are about nothing
exactly nothing
why should I fear exactly nothing

teach me to trust you more than my fantasies

First Hour of Morning (Lauds)

despite defects

we are stronger than we look
fearfully and wonderfully made
though my listening is impaired
I yet can hear a still small voice

though weak of heart
I can still steer through stormy seas
limp limbed yet I stretch the bow
tired eyed I find the target

I spring from the starting signal

Mid-morning—Third Hour (Terce)

the fruit is bruised

when the mouth speaks with conscience silent
with honorable interests compromised
the fruit is bruised
the hands stained

when promises are made too hastily
the effect is only hollow sounds
wasted shapes within a broken scaffold

teach me to listen to the conscience
you implanted in my heart

Noon — Sixth Hour (Sext)

the faces of those I love

old photographs tell new stories
such beautiful faces
especially hers
all seem now exquisite
viewed from distant time

Mid-afternoon — Ninth Hour (None)

this pleasant place you give

it is the evening of my life
though my vocation is far from spent
now I am free simply to be and try to understand my being
there is nothing more important I have yet to do
my mind has never been more full of deliberations
imaginations, arguments
moving like a breeze through every bend of the valley
my soul is one with mind and heart
while my body lags behind
strapped to my soul like a wounded animal

Evensong (Vespers)

help me not forget this evening

help me not forget this evening
the pure deep blue of the cloudless sky
reaching toward every mile of every visible light year

the sun is near to setting
yet still prairie hot
baking earth with fire

I love to be baked slowly in a warm sun
to become like a layer of the earth that's being glazed

since barefoot days my skin has loved
to soak up the late sun on the wide plains

Nighttime (Compline)

flow quietly

let the smoke and fury of the day smolder
cradled in a sighing lake
let birdsong yield to cricket speech
let brightness yield to subtle shades
let soft light glow into the night
like sleeping embers of an ardent fire

you have spent priceless energy on a sunny day
now let the river flow quietly to the sea

About the Author

Thomas C. Oden (PhD, Yale) is Henry Anson Buttz Professor of Theology and Ethics at Drew University and Director of the Center for Early African Christianity at Eastern University, St. Davids, PA. He is an ordained Methodist minister and the author of many books, including *The Rebirth of Orthodoxy: Signs of New Life in Christianity*, *How Africa Shaped the Christian Mind: Rediscovering the African Seedbed of Western Christianity*, *Doctrinal Standards in the Wesleyan Tradition*, *John Wesley's Scriptural Christianity: A Plain Exposition of His Teaching on Christian Doctrine*, and his three-volume work *Systematic Theology*.